T0318357

# *Entrepreneurship in the Gulf Cooperation Council*

# *Entrepreneurship in the Gulf Cooperation Council*

## *Guidelines for Starting and Managing Businesses*

Alexandrina Maria Pauceanu, PhD

AMSTERDAM • BOSTON • HEIDELBERG • LONDON
NEW YORK • OXFORD • PARIS • SAN DIEGO
SAN FRANCISCO • SINGAPORE • SYDNEY • TOKYO

Academic Press is an imprint of Elsevier

Academic Press is an imprint of Elsevier
125 London Wall, London EC2Y 5AS, United Kingdom
525 B Street, Suite 1800, San Diego, CA 92101-4495, United States
50 Hampshire Street, 5th Floor, Cambridge, MA 02139, United States
The Boulevard, Langford Lane, Kidlington, Oxford OX5 1GB, United Kingdom



**Notices**

Knowledge and best practice in this field are constantly changing. As new research and experience broaden our understanding, changes in research methods, professional practices, or medical treatment may become necessary.

Practitioners and researchers must always rely on their own experience and knowledge in evaluating and using any information, methods, compounds, or experiments described herein. In using such information or methods they should be mindful of their own safety and the safety of others, including parties for whom they have a professional responsibility.

To the fullest extent of the law, neither the Publisher nor the authors, contributors, or editors, assume any liability for any injury and/or damage to persons or property as a matter of products liability, negligence or otherwise, or from any use or operation of any methods, products, instructions, or ideas contained in the material herein.

**Library of Congress Cataloging-in-Publication Data**
A catalog record for this book is available from the Library of Congress

**British Library Cataloguing-in-Publication Data**
A catalogue record for this book is available from the British Library

ISBN: 978-0-12-811288-5

For information on all Academic Press publications
visit our website at https://www.elsevier.com/



*Publisher:* Nikki Levy
*Acquisition Editor:* Scott Bentley
*Editorial Project Manager:* Susan Ikeda
*Production Project Manager:* Jason Mitchell
*Designer:* Mark Rogers

Typeset by TNQ Books and Journals

**This book is dedicated to:**

- *Alexandru and Aurina Tucra, my lovely grandparents, in memoriam;*
- *My mother and my two nephews, Antonia and Maria;*
- *My friends from Sultanate of Oman—thank you for welcoming, supporting, and making me part of your families;*
- *My friends from Romania—rest assured I did not forget you;*
- *My CCBA family;*
- *All my past, present, and future students, wherever you are.*

# Contents

# Foreword

The Gulf Cooperation Council (GCC) economies are deeply dependent on the oil sector despite their efforts to diversify. The oil industry remains as their main source of fiscal revenues. A prolonged oil price slump will inevitably affect their economies. In this context, GCC governments have been eager to develop long-term sustainable economies diversified away from oil. This is done by developing a strong small and medium-sized enterprise (SME) sector. They have realized supporting the SME sector is less capital intensive, is quicker to execute, and generates added value faster.

The national economy of a country is, in fact, based on small and medium industries. These are the fundamentals, the foundations of all national economies. There is already a change we can see in the ecosystem in Oman. Nowadays a lot of young Omanis want to establish their own businesses. This was not the case a few years ago. This increased interest in the SME sector is advantageous for Oman not just because of the contribution it can make to the country's economy, but also for the important role it can play in bringing about job opportunities for Omani nationals.

In the Middle East countries and specially the GCC countries, the process of participation of the women in enterprise and businesses has been given due attention in the recent past. The long-term development strategy adopted by Oman has provided an encouraging environment for women entrepreneurs to participate and contribute toward this effect. Availability of education, training, and awareness has helped Omani women to emancipate in recent past and resultantly, Oman has a significant number of women entrepreneurs. Female entrepreneurship, and, in particular, the contribution of their ventures to aggregate economic activity, has gained increasing attention over recent years in Oman.

The author of this book has done intensive research on the subject and it will be highly beneficial for those budding entrepreneurs who venture into setting up SMEs. It has been enriched by more practical questions and expanded explanations with emphasis on entrepreneurship. It is evident that the book will provide essential guidelines for entrepreneurs. I feel honored and privileged to have this opportunity to write a foreword to this book.

**Ahmed Alawi Al Dhahab**
Chief Executive Officer
Salalah Mills Co. S.A.O.G.

# Acknowledgments

First of all, I would like to express my sincere thanks and profound gratitude to Sheikh Ahmed Alawi Al Dhahab (the CEO of Salalah Mills) who has been a source of continuous support, encouragement, and guidance. This work would not have been possible without his patronage and support. I would also like to acknowledge Sheikh Said bin Ali Al-Mashani (General Manager of Raysut Industrial Estate Salalah) for reviewing my work and giving me guidance, support, and motivation throughout this project.

I would like to extend my heartfelt gratitude to Mr. Salim Ali Mustahil Al Jabri for his extraordinary support and encouragement. My special thanks also to Mr. Mohammed Ahmed Al Ghassani (Manager of Public Authority for SMEs Development Salalah) for reviewing my work and encouraging me.

I would also like to express my gratitude and thanks to my esteemed colleagues Dr. Shouvik Sanyal, Dr. Mohammed Wamique Hisam, and Mrs. Shireen Rosario for reviewing and giving their valuable suggestions and feedback.

Last, but not the least, my gratitude and thanks to Susan Ikeda, my project manager, and Scott Bentley, the executive editor, for their support and guidance during publishing the book.

I can assure you this is only the first milestone of the road and I will continue to contribute to the development of Sultanate of Oman, my new home, through my knowledge, as much as I can.

**Alexandrina Maria Pauceanu, PhD**

# Introduction

*Formal education will make you a living; self-education will make you a fortune.*

***Jim Rohn***

We are living that particular moment in history when the economy is based on the exchange of information; we establish and operate businesses through communication of various kind of information transmitted in different ways.

The economic interest of Oman in GCC is mainly geared at securing the oil share in Gulf States in order to increase the capacity of supporting their own development program. In the context of oil crisis and rapid decline of oil and gas reserves volume, Sultanate of Oman is among the countries in GCC that have made significant efforts in promotion of innovation and entrepreneurship (Pauceanu, 2016b). As per April 23rd 2016, the country has a population of 4,422,602 inhabitants, among which 2,412,919 Omanis (NCSI, 2016), and gross national income (GNI) per capita of $19,002 (WorldBank, 2016). Oman is among the countries in GCC that have made significant efforts in promotion of innovation and entrepreneurship. The economic growth in Oman has been remarkable majorly due to increased earnings from oil and gas exports (Tlaiss, 2013). Oman has made a progress in ease of doing business classification, reaching 70th position in 2016, while in 2015 was ranked 77th position.

The long-term economy of the country is under the risk of decreasing oil reserves and increased exploration costs, triggering volatility of the oil prices. Additionally, the long-term search and continuous exploration of oil has been questioned, particularly in terms of carbon emission. The country is currently ranked in top 20 countries that have the highest level of carbon emission per capita (Darwish, 2014). Therefore, there is a great need to promote entrepreneurship in Oman and other GCC countries to curb issues of unemployment and carbon emission (Pauceanu, 2016b).

Small and medium enterprises (SMEs) are well-known to have a key role in promoting the economic sustainable growth of both the developing countries and already developed countries. SMEs' benefits have been echoed even outside realms of academia where funding bodies and analysts continue advocating to policy makers to promote development of SMEs in an effort to address the economic and social deprivation. Development of SMEs is important in creation of employment opportunities as they provide an environment where both the skilled and unskilled workforce can work together for the advancement of the society (Pauceanu, 2016a).

While development of SMEs remains a critical factor in many economies, the mode of doing business from idea conception to having an operational business, requires careful planning and adaptation to its specific environment.

Also the incentives related to foreign investments have become a major key factor in promoting business opportunities in economic zones (so-called free zones). There is a high competition among GCC countries in regard to attract foreign investors. Sultanate of Oman still has a long run in this direction, meanwhile United Arab Emirates and Qatar took a huge head start in this regard (Pauceanu, 2016a). Doha added an extra advantage in this regard through the international airport who has direct flights and connections all over the world and also by becoming a mark on World Trade Organization's agenda.

GCC countries (except Saudi Arabia) have plenty of similarities in regard to business ecosystem, socio-cultural and economic factors. This is the reason why the information contained in this book is applicable across GCC, with the required adaptation to specific context.

The concept and the basic entrepreneurial tools have been explained in this book. It is meant to be a guide for starting a business in GCC. The information presented in this book are essential to both start-ups and existing business owners. All the theories and information presented were adapted as much as possible to GCC-specific context.

*Entrepreneurship in the Gulf Cooperation Council: Guidelines for starting and managing businesses* is a pioneering work and nowadays there is no other comparable source of information available. The textbook has a practical-oriented approach and is addressed to all potential and existing entrepreneurs; it reflects as well author's opinion gained from years of practical experience in business and managerial consultancy (Europe and Middle East), academic, for-profit, and nonprofit sector.

**Alexandrina Maria Pauceanu, PhD**

*April 24, 2016*

*Salalah*

## Bibliography

Darwish, S. (2014). The Role of Universities in Developing Small and Medium Enterprises (SMEs): Future Challenges for Oman. *International Business and Management*, *8*(2), 70–77.

NCSI. (2016, February 20). *National Center for Statistics and Information*. Retrieved from https://www.ncsi.gov.om/Pages/NCSI.aspx.

Pauceanu, A. (2016a). Innovation and entrepreneurship in Sultanate of Oman - an empirical study. *Purushartha - A Journal of Management Ethics and Spirituality*.

Pauceanu, A. H. (2016b). Strategic Energy Management in Sultanate of Oman. *Montenegrin Journal of Economics*, *12*(1), 95–105.

Tlaiss, H. (2013). Women managers in the United Arab Emirates: successful careers or what?. Equality, Diversity and Inclusion. *An International Journal*, *32*(8), 756–776.

WorldBank. (2016, February 15). *Doing business*. Retrieved from http://www.doingbusiness.org/.

CHAPTER 1

# Introduction to Entrepreneurship

## Chapter Outline



**Entrepreneurship in the Gulf Cooperation Council.**

## Who Is an Entrepreneur?

The meaning of the term entrepreneur is an evolutionary one and is dependent on age and generation. In this case, when you consider Oman as an example, many young people still dream and wait for a government job. They prefer to have low-paid stable government jobs than to start a new enterprise and face the risk of failure. Within such context, the potential future leaders aspire to play a major key role, more than their precedents did. They are keen to conquer the areas that have been previously not explored. A part of today's generation is more adventurous. They have always dreamt of becoming leaders with vision and create their own distinct position within the turbulent economic environment for them to be successful entrepreneurs. To realize their goals, there is a great need to understand the actual meaning of an entrepreneur, its characteristics and the way to success.

An **entrepreneur** is a person who comes up with an idea and creates a new business amidst uncertainty and risk to achieve profits and growth opportunities, as well as assembles the necessary resources to capitalize on the identified opportunities (Barreto, 2013).

When a person initiates a decision to start a business, several factors have to be considered. Decision-making is key to all aspiring business owners. Great business decisions are critical to enable entrepreneurs reach their levels of success. After coming up with a business idea, there is a great need for the entrepreneur to test the business idea and as well to document and research all the aspects necessary to create and write down a feasibility study. If viable, a business plan should be drafted to outline the key business objectives, means of achieving the objectives, and timelines for the objectives.

## Concept of Entrepreneur, Entrepreneurship, and Enterprise

### Entrepreneur

Many people have always dreamt of becoming entrepreneurs for various reasons such as financial independence, need for freedom or just for being their own boss. Nevertheless, the road to entrepreneurship is characterized by several obstacles and entrepreneurs are required to take various risks and they can either win or fail. The move with their dreams acts as a major push for their success. To them, failure or success should not be a stop point; instead, it should be a motivator to achieve more and more successes. It is aid that success is like an addiction: as much as you will taste from it, the desire will become stronger.

An entrepreneur is derived from a French word "entreprendre," which means to undertake. This term was introduced in business in 1965 by Schumpeter, who was an Austrian economist. He launched the entrepreneurship field by associating it with Drucker's innovative definition of entrepreneurship as a systematic professional discipline. An entrepreneur will start an enterprise, search for opportunities or possible changes, and responds to it. Economists consider an entrepreneur as a fourth factor of production alongside capital, land, and labor. According to sociologists, entrepreneurs are innovators who draft new ideas for markets, techniques, and/or products. An entrepreneur will always perceive an opportunity, organize the required resources for exploitation of the opportunity, and exploit it.

An entrepreneur will always pay the price for the product to resell it at a certain higher price while making decision on how to obtain and use resources and at the same time admitting the risks involved.

An entrepreneur can be considered as an economic agent who will unite all factors of production to manufacture a product/service, incurs production costs, sells the product, and/or gets the profit by shifting the resources from lower into higher productivity and yield. Entrepreneurs will always be innovative and can use the process of shattering the status of the existing services and products to set up new or different services or products. According to Drucker, an entrepreneur will always look for changes, respond to them, and exploit any opportunity related therewith. Innovation is quoted as a critical tool for an entrepreneur where an entrepreneur will always convert source into a resource.

On the other hand, entrepreneurship can be considered as a process of coming up with something new/different and assuming the rewards and risks. The four aspects of being an entrepreneur include the following:

1. creation process
2. devotion of effort and time
3. being an entrepreneur
4. assuming the necessary risks.

*Personal Development for an Entrepreneur*

The entrepreneurial process begins with the entrepreneur himself/herself. They should be the mirror they would like to see in the community and should use the power of personal example. Given are qualities that are critical for personal development of an entrepreneur.

- *Spend time to get to know themselves*: An entrepreneur will spend a lot of time trying to know themselves. This helps in identifying own energy patterns and setting of the priorities right to achieve the goals set.
- *Spend time for personal growth*: Entrepreneurs know that to increase their personal worth, then they should first increase their net worth. This includes a lot of reading and studying to keep in pace with the trends in their industry, study what interests them, and understand the people they deal with; whether customers or employees.
- *Know the power of sharing*: Entrepreneurs will share and speak their ideas; they mentor people and share very essence of themselves. They know that they are single most critical component of their businesses.

*Personal Financial Management for an Entrepreneur*

Being a successful entrepreneur requires a lot of experience in managing personal finances. If you cannot manage your own personal budget, how can you manage your company budget? It is important to remember that company money is not your own personal pocket money. You and your company are two different entities and should be treated likewise.

**Practical exercise for financial management**: Take a notebook and write down all the income and the expenses you incurred in one month, does not matter how much small the income or the expense is. Write down the expenses on a daily basis. At the end of the first month, track down all the expenses and see where you spent more for things that you did not really need or expenses that are in excess. In the second month, write down again all your expenses and see if you have succeeded to improve your financial management.

**Tips**: If your expenses are more than your income, then put everything on the paper and identify the cause and solutions for it. If you can't manage extra income sources, then try to have better management with your other expenses from your budget. The golden rule is that you should be able to save at least 10% of your whole income on a monthly basis.

Returning to organization's budget, there are five ways (also known as DPSEP) through which one can manage the finances; this could include the following:

- *Diversification*: They say that an entrepreneurial venture has higher chances of failing than succeeding. Therefore, by diversifying and investing in another side of business or alternate investments gives one the breathing room in event one business is not performing as expected.
- *Plan for "bad days"*: Business does not always perform all year round. An informed entrepreneur will budget the personal finances to have something to draw during the leaner months so as to cover for essentials like utilities, insurance, and rent.
- *Separate personal money from business money*: It is a good idea for an entrepreneur to keep business finances separate from personal finances. This gives the business more credibility, increases sense of legitimacy, and helps in reducing personal liability if something negative happens.
- *Ensure expenses are below income*: Expenses will always rise to meet income. Therefore, ensure that expenses are always below the income by estimating your income.
- *Protect your most valuable asset*: Some entrepreneurs may overlook the need for disability insurance. It is always good to ensure that your most valuable persons or assets are taken care off in event your income stops. You can do this in many ways, like, for example, savings, private insurance, pensions, etc.

## Entrepreneurship

Entrepreneurship entails innovation, decision-making, implementation, independency, and forecasting of the future and success. It can be viewed as a discipline founded on knowledge-based theory. It is as a result of complex socioeconomic, psychological, legal, technological, and other factors. It is a dynamic and risky process that involves fusion of capital, human talent, and technology. Entrepreneurship is applicable to both small and big businesses and to noneconomic and economic activities (Jayawarna, Jones, & Macpherson, 2015).

Different entrepreneurs may possess similar traits, though each one is unique in a way. From the various studies conducted by the main author in this field in Sultanate of Oman, it is obvious that potential entrepreneurs can learn the successful entrepreneurship behavior from their mentors (Pauceanu, 2016).

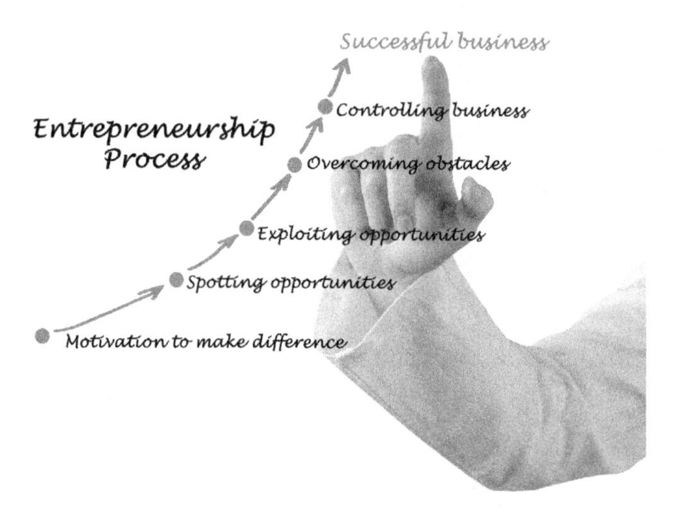


In itself, entrepreneurship can be considered as a process that is free of stray incidents. It is organized and purposeful search for change that should be conducted after a systematic analysis of the business opportunities. Entrepreneurship is a philosophy as it depends on how a person thinks and acts, meaning that it can exist in any government or business environment, science and technology, education, and poverty eradication among others.

Entrepreneurship can be defined as an action or a process taken by an entrepreneur to establish an enterprise. The process is creative in nature. The entrepreneur builds and creates something virtually from scratch. It is a knack of sensation where others see contradiction, chaos, and confusion. It is the attitude of the mind to exploit opportunities, take calculated risks, and consequently derive the benefits of establishing the venture. This may involve numerous activities involved in creation, conception, and operation of an enterprise. This dynamic process that entails change, vision, and creation and requires an application of passion and energy toward implementation and creation of innovative ideas and solutions. Critical ingredients of entrepreneurship involve willingness to undertake calculated risks on basis of equity, time, or career as well as the ability to form an effective venture team.

### *Enterprise*

Entrepreneurship is a process of creation by an entrepreneur who starts an enterprise. In this case, the entrepreneur becomes the actor while entrepreneurship is the act. Enterprise is therefore the outcome of act and the actor.

Therefore, an enterprise can be defined as a business organization that provides good and/or services, contributes to national income, and creates jobs for economic development (Rice, 2013).

## *Decision to be an Entrepreneur*

Being an entrepreneur and successfully running a business are two totally different things (Bell, 2014). Despite the fact that we certainly are in need for more employers, business ownership is not just for anyone. Making a decision to be an entrepreneur is among the hardest decisions that require courage, patience, and confidence.

To avoid dilemma on what should be done, learn to make decision as an entrepreneur. When starting a business, one needs to prepare for the start-up both financially and emotionally, and be committed to the constant needs up to maturity. A move to start a business requires one to make very critical decisions. Making the decisions should not be underestimated. Great business decisions are the main things that enable entrepreneurs reach their levels of success. Once a person comes with a business idea, a business plan is critical. Some of the key questions that an entrepreneur needs to understand before undertaking any business include the following:

1. Does the business idea have the features that can attract investors?
2. How much capital are you willing to invest?
3. Is the business's track record clean enough to allow all forms of financial help?

As an entrepreneur, the most important task is to create a huge customer base and ensure a high retention power. Decision-making will normally engage you to take action. Decisions are critical in determining the effectiveness of execution and success of the business thereof.

One of the most challenging decisions of an entrepreneur is to determine what business to do and how to do it. From the author's experience, potential entrepreneurs think that they should do something completely different, something that it was not done before. In their opinion, this will ensure their success. As a result, because they cannot think of something completely new, they stuck themselves in this point. My advice for them was to do things differently. A lot of people cannot still make the difference between these two extremely important issues in entrepreneurship: *doing different things* or *doing things differently*. Frequently, people use these terms as if they have the same meaning. So it is important to clarify these two terms.

*Doing different things* means doing something completely different. For example, if someone is producing toothpaste, doing different things would mean for someone else to produce toothbrushes or electronics.

*Doing things differently* refers to the fact that several providers are offering the same service, but one of them is more creative and offers the same service but "dressed" better. For example, if we have two medical doctors that provide the same services, but one is more creative and "dresses up" the office in such manner that will not look like a clinic or hospital. In this way, the creative one offers more mental comfort to the patients.

So, now, *creativity* is the "word of the day." The creative entrepreneur will be the most successful one with growth potential and further development. For a better understanding, it must be mentioned that the innovation is the output of creativity. So, as an entrepreneur, your creativity is your only limitation.

## Reasons to Become an Entrepreneur

Many people believe that entrepreneurs are majorly driven by the desire to have big money. Money is just one of the reasons why one should become an entrepreneur. Given are 10 reasons why a person becomes an entrepreneur.

1. **Opportunity**: An entrepreneur can decide what he/she wants the work to be like, what to do, and what the mecca is for him/her. In simple terms, entrepreneurship allows one to explore various ventures and decide on what to work on.
2. **Autonomy**: Some entrepreneurs are motivated by the need to break the daily grind that normally results from a career that is not self-sustaining. Fear of failure is what motivates some entrepreneurs to keep going as there feel that going corporate way turns them into a robot.
3. **Freedom**: Some people become entrepreneurs for them to be able to call their own shots, have the ability to set their own life, and be in charge of their destiny.

4. **Responsibility to the Society**: For some people, the societal issues act as the major drivers for their work. Entrepreneurs should always analyze the state of the world and examine the stories that play out at macro or global level. While striving to make sense of the big picture, they look for places of passion and personal strength so that to have an impact on the world.
5. **Impact**: An entrepreneur will work knowing that each action taken has a direct impact to the business. An employee will have a limited impact but an entrepreneur can break or make the business from whatever he/she does.

6. **Family**: Some entrepreneurs are driven by the desire to have enough time with their families. In most cases, an entrepreneurship is flexible and can be practiced at most convenient time.
7. **Change**: Some people engage into entrepreneurship to make something more efficient or better than it is.
8. **Legacy**: Some people are motivated by the desire to leave a personal legacy.
9. **Accomplishment**: A sense of accomplishment makes some entrepreneurs truly happy. This implies putting more efforts everyday to accomplish the goals of building a successful venture.
10. **Control**: Some people are motivated by the sense of security resulting from being in complete control of the work, or security or being in control of their own destiny.

## Characteristics of an Entrepreneur

Given are characteristics of an entrepreneur:

1. Creativity and innovation
   Creativity and innovation entails the impulse of mind that triggers the concept of establishing a base plan. The idea should be *innovative* in actual sense. Nevertheless, there is

possibility of generating a new idea of an old innovation, which is still considered as creative and innovative. An innovative idea can turn someone into an entrepreneur. One should not let their business innovation strategy come with endless string of ideas. Barreto (2013) notes that thoughts can be easily turned into actions through the following:

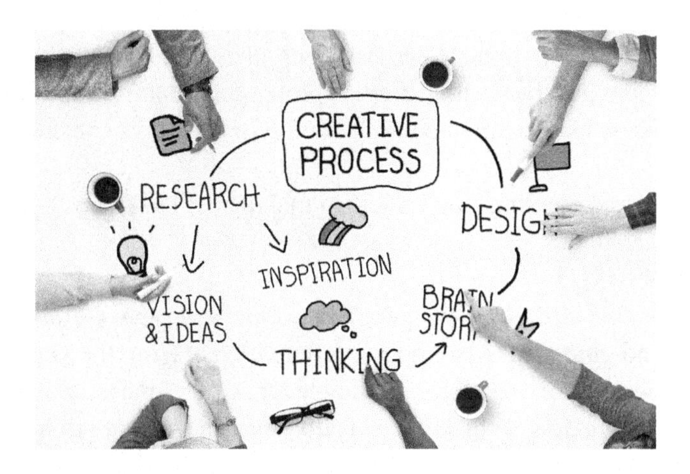


a. *Ideas and Innovation*: Generation of ideas forms the first process in any innovation. There is no idea that is of lesser importance. Engage as many people as possible so as to gather ideas from different minds, both externally and internally, even from competitors.
b. *Incubation*: The best ideas should be incubated by developing a concept in paper to consult with stakeholders. Incubation can be effective in rolling out ideas.
c. *Implementation*: After incubating the best ideas, it is appropriate to focus on specific issues or solution, or set of sensible parameters as well as implementing the idea fully.
d. *Sustain or exit*: This forms the final step in any innovation process where the entrepreneur choses either to sustain the project or exit. Innovation may not go on forever. It is advisable that one either develop a transition plan to exit or stabilize it to embed it to the daily operations.

2. Self-motivation

Given are things that an aspiring entrepreneur should do:

a. Start the business in the area of expertise.
b. If one does not have the expertise, then one can tie up with the target company and get as much experience as possible or such for strong networks with specific target industry that will help in liaising with people who have been in that business for quite sometime.

   c. Hire experts or specialized consultants in those area where you need support, one can also search mentors or advisors at the government entities, which are specialized in developing and promoting entrepreneurial activities.
3. Family support
   A focused family support is crucial and critical for any successful entrepreneur.
   a. In any case, one has to convince the family on any impending move. It is imperative to know that the family can impede and hamper with the business.
   b. If one fails to convince the family, there is probability that in future, confidence in doing the business may be affected as the family will always consider it with emotions.
   c. Family support and blessings are critical in making the next steps and rising up the entrepreneurial ladder.
4. Value experience
   Always show positive attitude to the people working with you. Get a mentor from which you can find guidance. Also, do not ignore advice from the people around you irrespective of their age, experience, or knowledge. Cope up easily and very fast with age limit to enable one to synchronize and add your years of age to other people years of experience.

   Remember that you cannot fully understand right or wrong experience or knowledge without success or failure.
5. Financing
   Studies show that financing is a problem for start-ups (Alalawi & Alali, 2015). To overcome financing issues, one should do the following:
   a. Start depositing whatever the amount that is available from the time you decide that you will be an entrepreneur.
   b. Source for funds from other sources so that cumulatively you may have enough money for the business.
   c. You can source for funds upfront and try to get a small amount on credit so that slowly by slowly the amount can increase and you can use it to expand the business.
   d. Before taking any money from the bank, ensure that you only take the amount that you are capable of paying back.
6. Redundancy
   An entrepreneur should have backup plans. They are the following:
   a. calculate alternative scope in case there is failure to comply with the target;
   b. think upfront on how to restand in vent of failure and the capacity to cope up with the unwanted situation.
7. Marketing challenge
   Any business calls for the ability to focus and market the product. This requires critical understanding of the client and may require use of:

a. *Social networking*: Social networking is currently used by many people as mainstream medium for business promotion. A broader network acts as an opening for new opportunities. Social networking can be critical in creating product awareness.
b. *Learning from all*: It is necessary that one be prepared mentally to learn from every opportunity that comes by your way. Ensure that you learn from real-life experiences as opportunities may not come more than once.
c. *Listening*: Have patient to listen and attend to others. A successful entrepreneur will always listen carefully and not talk unnecessarily. Any move to attentively listening to others is an avenue to win the attention of that person.
d. *Presentation skills*: Presentation acts as a critical component in any business. If one can overcome faltering and fumble, as well as present the message in a smart way, there are consequent gains. Be spontaneous, be frank, and be prepared. It is critical to practice beforehand on the message you would like to convey before any big meeting. A successful presenter will always synchronize the content and time precisely and will prepare the presentation using strong and convincing words. There is also need to maintain order and ensure lively voice.

8. Technology and network
   a. *Technology*: Smart and proper use of technology will always keep one ahead of the others. Ensure that the technological equipment used is modern. This includes mobile phones, laptop, web browsing, and email operation.
   b. *Networking gift*: This is a promo or AdSense sent to the target network to capture their attention as well as making you to outstand from the competitors.

c. *Use of networking*: Try to increase the current network and maintain the already existing networks. Ensure that they are well conversant with your status. Take advantage of your networking linkage.

9. Target revenue
   In start-ups, the initial phase may be characterized by huge losses in revenue and this may sometimes even collapse the initial capital flow. Nevertheless, at the end, the entrepreneur must ensure minimum revenue target, which is the essence of survival of the business. The minimum target of revenue set should be achievable. This ensures the existence of the business and allows gradual taking of risks as well as enable one to think big in the long run.
10. Personal branding
   Personal branding is critical to start-ups. This can be created by developing a unique logo, visiting card, or design pad to reflect all sorts of scope of your business. You can use mobile phone as a resource hub to enable you to run the business from any place.
11. Overcome failure

Frank Sinatra used to say, "The best revenge is massive success." Failure is inevitable but real heroes will never collapse. The shortest way to handle failure is by reframing of the mind by trying to look at situations from different dimensions.

- It is critical to get feedback from trustworthy persons. Always seek perspectives from persons who might not have been supportive rather than seeking support that only feeds your ego.
- Revise your strategies and be open to ideas that will propel you forward. Allow people to speak and note carefully their feedback.
- Refocus by overcoming that feeling of failure and embracing the new path to your success.
- It is good to be prepared always for failure and ensure you turn it into success. There is likelihood of facing natural calamities, betrayal from partners, mismatch with the

supplies, and capital shortage among others, never give up. Always reassess your strategies and plan to take action.

**How to overcome failure**

a. *Stop entertaining loser mindset.* The more you worry about losing, the more likely you are to lose.
b. *Assess failure, face the facts*: Glossing over something that went wrong or even discussing the events that did not work will never help the people involved learn from the past mistakes.
c. *Define the roles clearly*: Establishing clear accountability is critical self-policing ethics in the workplace.
d. *Welcome feedback from employees*: Give your employees the voice to solve the problems and differences in the company. This ensures that they work hard to succeed.
e. *Encourage the team to deliver in their roles*: Always demonstrate to the employees the importance of quality when dealing with the clients. For instance, eliminating grammar and spelling mistakes in all documentation is very critical.
f. *Emphasize the values of the team*: Print and post the company values everywhere in the premises. This acts as a constant reminder.
g. *Always lead by example*: Leading by example is not just a catchy phrase. Always note that employees will be watching and may be influenced by the way one treats the coworkers and customers.
h. *Celebrate the success with the team members*: Celebrating normally reminds employees that you believe in their work and ability to overcome any adversity.

## Theories of Entrepreneurship

These are propositions by people on entrepreneurship and entrepreneur. These include the following:

### Economic Theories

These theories date back to first half of 1700s from the works of Cantillon Richard who referred entrepreneurs as risk takers. These include the Austrian Market, Classic and Neoclassical schools of thought that focus mostly on economic conditions and opportunities created. The economic theories of entrepreneurship receive criticisms for their failure to recognize open and dynamic nature of market systems. They ignore the uniqueness of entrepreneurial activity and downplay the diverse contexts within which entrepreneurship occurs (Barreto, 2013).

### Resource-Based Theories

These theories focus on leveraging of resources by individuals to attain the entrepreneurial efforts off the ground. The accessibility to capital enhances the opportunity of getting new ventures off the ground though entrepreneurs will in most cases start ventures with very little capital. Some of other resources that entrepreneurs should leverage include social networks and human resources like education. In some instances, intangible elements of leadership added by an entrepreneur to the mix acts as irreplaceable resources (Barreto, 2013).

### Psychological Theories

These are theories that focus on the emotional and mental elements of an individual. These theories were first put forward by David McClelland who is a psychologist and professor at Harvard. According to the theories, people having strong internal control locus believe that their actions can easily influence the external world. According to the research by Barreto (2013), most entrepreneurs have strong internal control locus. Also, these theories confirm that resilience, creativity, and optimism play a major role in driving the entrepreneurial behavior (Barreto, 2013).

### Anthropological/Sociological Theories

Sociological theories center their explanation of entrepreneurship on various social contexts that facilitate leveraging for entrepreneurs. These contexts include desire for meaningful life, social networks, social–political environment, and ethnic identification. Anthropological theories approach the entrepreneurship by using a context of culture and evaluating how the cultural forces like social attitudes influence the perception of people on entrepreneurship and entrepreneurial behaviors (Barringer, 2012).

### Opportunity-Based Theory

This theory was introduced by Peter Drucker in 1985. He contends that entrepreneurs succeed when they notice the opportunities created by technological, cultural, and social changes and takes advantage of them. For instance, a business that caters for older people may consider a sudden influx of youngsters in their target area as a threat to their business but an entrepreneur will consider this as an opportunity to open a club (Barringer, 2012).

**Case Example: Ibn Khaldun**

Ibn Khaldun is a Muslim thinker born in Tunisia. His writings on economics, economic-oriented policies, and economic surplus remain relevant in the world of today just as they were during his time. He opposed the involvement of State in production and trade activities by arguing that bureaucrats cannot understand the world of commerce and do not possess the same motivation as businessmen.

In economics, Ibn Khaldun systematically analyzed the importance of technology and functioning and specialization of the economy. He is considered as the first economist in Arab world. His economic theory constitutes the framework of his history. There is no one who has ever proposed a theory that explicitly explains and predicts rise and fall of nations, empires, and civilization. He describes the best State as the one with minimal bureaucracy, minimal taxation, and minimum mercenary.

His explanation on economic surplus and specialization depicts specialization as a key source of economic surplus. An environment that is conducive for specialization increases the commitment of an entrepreneur to production and trade. He says,

> *Each particular kind of craft needs persons to be in charge of it and skilled in it. The more numerous the various subdivisions of a craft are, the larger the number of the people who (have to) practice that craft. The particular group (practicing that craft) is colored by it. As the days follow one upon the other, and one professional coloring comes after the other, the crafts-coloring men become experienced in their various crafts and skilled in the knowledge of them. Long periods of time and the repetition of similar (experiences) add to establishing the crafts and to causing them to be firmly rooted.*

For Ibn Khaldun, when there is law, order, and security of peace, then it is possible to realize greater specialization when there is a large population with minimal taxation and operating in free trade without restriction or impediment. On the other hand, his colleague, Adam Smith, argues that specialization can be considered as a function of market.

## *Sociocultural Environment and Entrepreneurship*

In broad terms, the sociocultural environment comprises of the culture and social system of the people. This mainly entails the intangible elements created by man that affect the behavior, perception, relationship, and way of life of people. A sociocultural environment consists of all the conditions, elements, and influences that shape the personality of a person and potentially affect their disposition, decision, attitude, and behavior. These include values, beliefs, habits, lifestyles, and forms of behaviors developed from educational, religious, and social and cultural conditioning. Such elements are learned, shared, and transmitted from generation to generation (Blank, 2013).

Therefore, in relation to entrepreneurship, sociocultural environment can be defined as consisting of elements of culture and social system of the people that negatively or positively influence and affect entrepreneural behavior, emergence, performance, and development in general. Such elements condition the values, actions, and thinking of a person with respect to entrepreneurship and forms the sociocultural environment of entrepreneurship (Emerson, 2016).

### *Case Study: Taleem Training and Skills Development Center, UAE*

The vision of Taleem Center says everything about its purpose: "Taleem Training and Skills Development Center—Empowering and enriching the learning process and supporting individuals with learning challenges in achieving their full potential to be positive contributors to the development of their society." This is a new type of entity in Gulf Cooperation Council (GCC) area and it was set by Ms. Shereen Al Nowais. Shereen obtained her masters degree in the art of communication from Zayed University in Abu Dhabi.

There is an old saying that applies here also—"The need is your best teacher"; so the saying applies itself in this situation also. Shereen created Taleem Training and Skills Development Center because her own son had a learning difficulty (dyslexia) and she wanted to reach out to the UAE community to bring awareness about it to other parents who might be in similar situations.

"I felt it was my responsibility as a mother to raise the awareness on learning disabilities, identification, treatment and ways to deal with it. I believed in my heart that by founding Taleem Training and Skills Development Center, I could provide also the much needed relief to parents, training to teachers, assessments to learners and evaluation programs to educational institutions" says Shereen.

Taleem Center is a community service initiative oriented toward sustainable community development with a long-lasting and positive impact on the well-being of all segments of the Abu Dhabi community. The necessity to support children, teenagers, and students suffering from learning disabilities in Abu Dhabi and all the Emirates led me to establish this center. It is important to note that the work of the center is aligned with Abu Dhabi Education Council's vision of reaching the level of teaching success that competes on a global scale. Taleem Center opened in February 8, 2014 with only 16 students. After a year of operation, the number of students has risen to over 800 being served by our expert training specialists.

"As a mother, I personally went through the turmoil of seeing my own son getting frustrated and feeling helpless when it came to study and school. After plenty of search, I found my answer in the USA. So my son was diagnosed with dyslexia by the specialists over there. Through several intervention strategies provided in the USA, my son was then able to overcome dyslexia and his learning difficulties. Upon returning to the UAE, the next step became obvious for me: to help others who are facing the same issues to find their path and to coach families how to support their loved ones who are facing learning difficulties. So the outcome was Taleem Training and Skills Development Center!" tells Shereen.

The Center is a privately owned and funded organization; it is just in the second year of operation, so it maintains funds to pay the salaries of instructional specialists and staff. The main goal is to meet the needs of the clients in need and students with learning disabilities, so as long as they are serving the needs of the UAE community in regard to learning difficulties, they are satisfied with this outcome versus the financial outcome.

Shereen also says that if she would have to start all over again, she would seek more government support and funding. Her advice for anyone wishing to start their own business, they must do it because of the love and passion they have for meeting the needs of their clients and making an impact on the world and their community. When Shereen is talking about her fears and difficulties from the start of the road and how she overcomes it, she says "I've always stayed positive and believed passionately in meeting the needs of students, clients, and the UAE culture. Because I remained positive and truly believed that I was making a difference in the lives of students with learning difficulties, this in itself made most of my fears disappear."

Taleem Training and Skills Development Center, Al Morour Road, Al Nahyan Camp Area, Office 503; PO Box 115004, Abu Dhabi; Telephone: + 971 2 4441100; Fax +971 2 4441101; Email: askus@taleemcentre.com.

## *Women Entrepreneurs in Gulf Cooperation Council*

Most women in GCC are literate and have made considerable achievements in education front. Currently, the adult literacy in GCC stands at 84% among women. They have a better talent pool than their male counterparts (Bilal & Al Mqbali, 2015).

Nevertheless, the female labor participation in GCC is very low and lies at 26.9%, which is half of the world's average (Figs. 1.1 and 1.2). The lower participation of women in

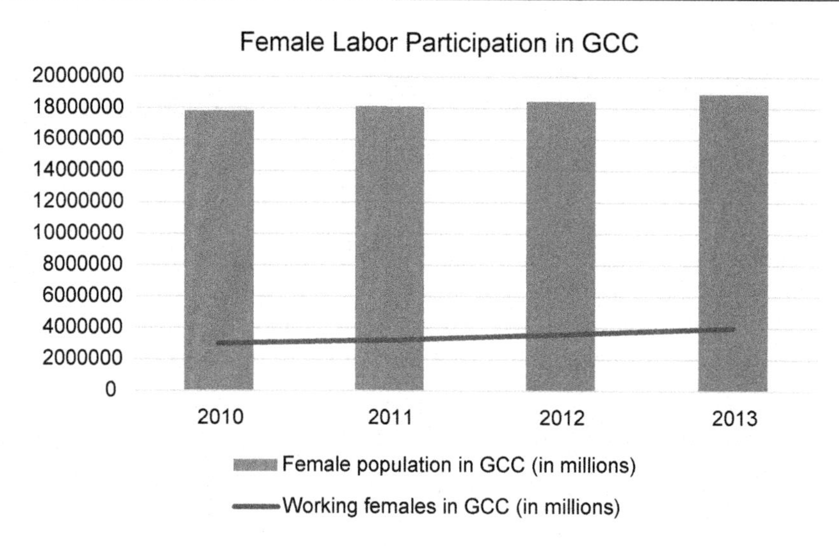


**Figure 1.1**
Adaptation from the World Bank, Al Masah Capital Research, 2013.

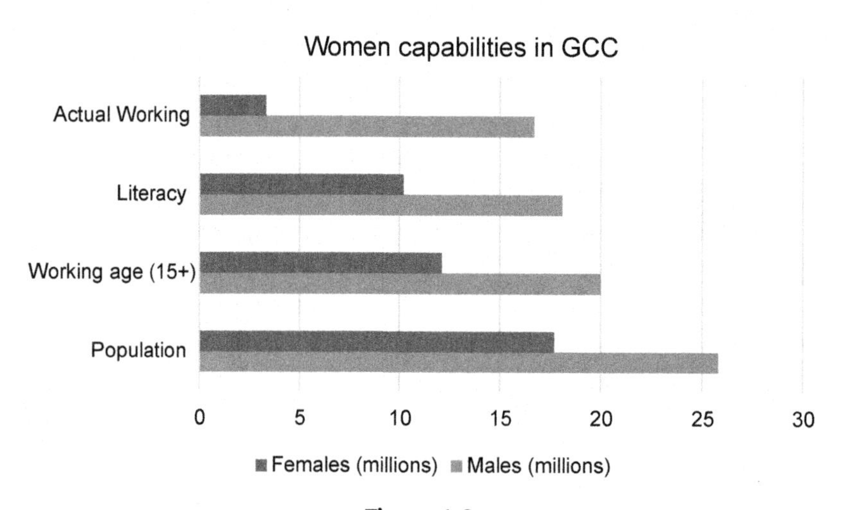


**Figure 1.2**
Adaptation after women capability in Gulf Cooperation Council. *World Bank, Al Masah Capital Research, 2015.*

workforce is mainly attributed to sociocultural restrictions and customs that exist in most GCC countries. Most of the countries in GCC give women right to work but in proper environment only when a woman is not required to mix with men.

In author's opinion, women have more chances to succeed in business than the men, because they are already having the basic management skills from home, where they need to deal and manage with various tasks. Also, studies show that women are more attentive to details and more decided to succeed in business.

Other countries like Saudi Arabia restrict the women from traveling, marrying, divorce, or working without consent of the male guardian, mostly a father, brother, husband, or even a son. Subsequently, out of the 10.2 million literate women, only 3.3 million are in employment. The rest 6.9 million are unemployed (Ennis, 2015).

This untapped pool of literate women is a huge loss to the society and economy of GCC at large. This has compelled the governments to consider this and concrete steps have been taken to handle such issues. For instance, the Saudi government has reserved 75% of the jobs created to women while in Oman, women are being supported to start their own businesses by being funded, educated on entrepreneurship and are becoming empowered economically.

**Omani Serial Entrepreneur**

Qais Al-Khonji is a serial entrepreneur in Sultanate of Oman. Being an entrepreneur in a country with only three million citizens as your potential clients may require critical analysis of the target customer and the product requirement. Qais Al-Khonji has admitted to having failed in his first start-up since he never conducted the market research and failed to follow a lean methodology that involves careful analysis and resting of the approach to use based on the market response.

Nevertheless, Al-Khonji embraced his failure and started another project. He says, "I try and learn even though this means losing. I consider the benefits to be in learning and failure a step towards success."

Al-Khonji is not just an entrepreneur you encounter during entrepreneurship events. He has had five start-ups in the last 3 years and embraced failure in most of them with only one succeeding. Business is his life! He has always gotten up and started all over again upon failure. Al-Khonji is a perfect example of what the entrepreneurs in Gulf are likely to face, especially from family business.

Al-Khonji comes from a wealthy family that operates real estate business in UK, Sultanate of Oman. In Sultanate of Oman goes by the name Mohamed and Ahmed Al-Khonji.

The 32 years old Mohamed and Ahmed Al-Khonji have been working as a banker and adviser of four of his father's companies. In 2010, he made a decision to engage himself in entrepreneurship and he launched his first company by the name Qais United Agency. His company dealt with selling and importation of water filtration systems from China to Sultanate of Oman. The business closed down in mid-2011, after 18 months due to poor returns.

In 2012, he started four ventures at a go. He was offering services in various sectors like health tourism, education, digital meters for electricity and water, and electrical freezing technology. From the four ventures, three failed.

Currently, he is working with the digital meter company and he hopes to build it up to long-term business. He notes that the business may take time to pick up and start generating revenue. Al-Khonji also works as a reseller for Thermax company, which is an Indian company in Oman. His plans are underway for launching solar products.

*Continued*

**Omani Serial Entrepreneur—cont'd**

The decision to shift from family business to a totally new entrepreneurial venture is not a decision that happens overnight. Some of the few lessons to learn from Al-Khonji's story include the following:

1. **Be focused**: Never give up, whenever you fail in any start-up, embrace failure, and move to the next step.
2. **Market research is crucial**: Al-Khonji admitted that he followed his passion and skills but did not study the market needs clearly. Always assess the market needs clearly and an exciting idea may not be necessarily enough if people are not hungry for it.
3. **Know your customer well**: Al-Khonji admitted that the first start-up failed because he imported products that did not survive in the market. This was majorly because of the monopoly and small nature of Omani market, and also the service company is a low hanging fruit in Oman. It is good to test the customers' appetite for the product before launching it.
4. **Know yourself**. Launching something that you want to build and something that is demanded by the market are two different things. At times you may have so much passion in doing something until you forget what the market demands. Nevertheless, it is much better to have passion for that which you intend to build.

At his core, Al-Khonji is an inspiring entrepreneur. He has been advising people to be focused, patient, and courageous. "Try more than once before you give up, and be very focused on your work," he says. "I like to try and learn even though this means losing, the benefit is in learning and failure is a step towards success."

In venturing into entrepreneurship by leaving the comfort of his family business and by refusing to be phased out by failure, Al-Khonji is a perfect example to follow for all those who are aspiring to make changes in the entrepreneurial field.

## *Practical Steps to Become an Entrepreneur: Case Study From Sultanate of Oman*

## *Business Start-Up*

### *Steps in Business Start-Up*

There has been a misconception by many people about business. Some believe that starting a business is very simple and involves just making a decision to start a venture without necessarily having proper knowledge. Others consider it as rocket science, very hard task. Nevertheless, there are various types of businesses. For instance, some people may engage in service delivery while other may produce goods and sell them to make profits. Any person who uses his/her brains to produce goods is an entrepreneur (Al-Sadi, Belwal, & Al-Badi, 2013).

The success in any business is dependent on various things such as business rules, regulations, strategies, and policies. Before engaging in any business, it is imperative that a person be acquainted with these skills. This needs proper decision-making and planning, guidance, and resources. A clear and detailed business plan is critical to an entrepreneur to gradually achieve the target. Assets and capital may be important for any start-up but may not be the main factors. Starting a business without proper guidance exposes one to investment risks (Blank, 2013).

Another important element, which might contribute to the success of a business is the company's name. Choosing a suitable name for the business can be stressful and difficult. Any investor would like to see his/her own name as a forefront for a company. Research studies show that businesses who let the customer know what they are all about from the name are more successful (for example, Salalah Mills, Sadim Business Consulting, Dhofar University, etc.). It is recommendable to choose a business name that is easy to remember and easy to be pronounced. One should also consider to check if the name you choose for your company has an Internet domain available (this thing will save you from frustrations later on).

Location, based on the type of business you plan to do, plays also a vital role in the success of your future business. So choosing the right location with suitable facilities is vital for any entrepreneur.

Any person aspiring to be an entrepreneur should know how the business is started. This implies the need for clear thoughts on trade license, letter of credit (LC) opening, machinery, company registration, and account opening among others. Entrepreneurs should have a clear idea of the products to be sold, marketing, modes if paying taxes, and means of transport amongst others. Given are the steps in starting a business (Rice, 2013) (Fig. 1.3).

*Step 1: Make a Decision*

Any person aspiring starting a business should seriously think about the venture and be mentally prepared on how to do business. This requires one to make a very firm and informative decision. Aimless decision can never lead to a specific goal.

*Step 2: Decision on the Form of Business*

After making the decision to start a business, an aspiring businessperson should select the form of business to engage in, for instance, the business can be manufacturing, trading and supplies, commission based, imports or exports. It is critical to ensure that the business that is started is market demand oriented.

*Step 3: Decision on Joint Venture, Limited Company, or Sole Proprietorship*

It is critical for a person to evaluate the capacity to carry out the business alone as sole proprietorship or through partnership. If the person is capable, then the business can be ran as sole proprietorship though at times this appears to be very tough to engage in all activities and complicacy. Also, the person can look for an honest, integrated, and successful individual and start the business as a partnership. There may be need to expand the company to either private

**STEP 1 –Name reservation**

The Ministry of Commerce and Industry (MCI) must approve the name of the business entity. For those business entities who have certain words included in their name (for example Oman) the MCI requires a higher starting capital.

**STEP 2 – Ministry of Commerce and Industry application**

This part involves preparing and obtaining specific documents, accordingly to the type of business entity that will be established. You might need also a bank statement from a local bank to prove the compliance with capital requirements.

**STEP 3 – Chamber of Commerce and Industry Registration**

The final part of the registration process of the business entity.

**STEP 4 – Approvals**

Depending on the type of business entity and intended business activities, further governmental approvals might be required.

**STEP 5 – Other permits that might be needed**

Depending on the type of business entity and business activities, you might need to obtain: a municipality license; tax registration; registration with the Police; registration with the Ministry of Manpower, to apply for labor; clearances and visas; import/export license, depending on the nature of the business; industrial, environmental and other permits and licenses, depending on the nature of the business.

**Figure 1.3**
General legal steps to register a business entity in Gulf Cooperation Council.

or public limited through incorporation. The choice lies with the individual aspiring to start the business.

*Step 4: Choice of a Business Name*

Any type of the business that a person decides to start will have to have a business name. A good name is an avenue to mileage of business. In partnership, all the parties involved should jointly choose the name. A person can incorporate the company with the names chosen previously before incorporation.

*Step 5: Business Location*

A well-oriented entrepreneur will emphasize on a proper location for the business, hence need for proper selection of the site. A good location will determine the targeted consumers, labor availability, and machine and equipment setup. Statistics reveal that many consumers who are business oriented often flourish in areas of different popular markets.

*Step 6: License and Other Documentation*

A trade license is an indicator of the acceptability of the person to run the business. Any business without a trade license is illegal. It is critical for the businessperson to collect all the required documents before starting the business.

*Step 7: Business TIN and Bank Accounts*

The business TIN (Taxpayer Identification Number) and bank accounts are crucial for any business. As an entrepreneur at the beginning of the road, you should take a look at the commissions, costs, and benefits you might be able to receive from your partner bank.

## Myths on Entrepreneurship

Many people have different beliefs on entrepreneurship. Somehow, the entrepreneurship idea has been grounded upon legend, movies, anecdotes, and who-knows-what else. Some of the major ones are outlined below.

1. Entrepreneurs do not quit
   It is unfortunate that some people believe that entrepreneurs do not quit and portray quitting as bad. Fact to be told, quitting is the one that defines an entrepreneur. In most cases, entrepreneurs have to quit their employment and wages to become entrepreneurs. This is the first quitting point. Also, some entrepreneurs have to quit their ventures, especially if one realizes that the business is turning out to be crappy. Reputable entrepreneurs like Steve Jobs and Elon Musk quit at some point. These are the rockstars of entrepreneurship. This shatters the idea that entrepreneurs never quit. Successful entrepreneurs need to quit at some point. Quitting from something not worthwhile is not wrong. True success is measured by how to quit, what to quit, and when to quit.
2. Entrepreneurs are aware of what exactly they want and know how to go for it
   The fact is many entrepreneurs have no idea on how to achieve their goals. Entrepreneurship can be considered as a process of trial, failure, another trial, success, and trial again and again. In most cases, entrepreneurs do not know what to do and they are compelled to follow their guts.
3. An entrepreneur is his/her own boss
   No one can be his/her own boss. Everyone has to report to someone. Any person with complete control of the business will have the business as the boss. If the business is consultancy, the clients are the bosses and if the business is funded by investors, then the

investors are the bosses. In most cases, the business may not even allow one a work–life balance.

4. Entrepreneurs should be connected
There is a famous saying that goes around, “it doesn’t matter what you know; it matters who you know.” An entrepreneur is advised to shun such believes. If this was true, then the first-generation immigrants would not be considered as entrepreneurs as most of them were. Some unconnected entrepreneurs like Andrew Groove from Intel and Jerry Yang from Yahoo are foreign-born entrepreneurs who started business from scratch without any assistance from anyone. Entrepreneurs who are quick to realize that connectedness is a myth will in most cases rely on their own determination and grit rather than on some star-studded safety haven. This motivates them to start companies and to successfully run them.
5. Entrepreneurs are normally rich
Some entrepreneurs are rich though they certainly did not start rich. In fact, even when the business is in full operation, entrepreneurs are not normally the fat cats that many people think they are. A study by American Express showed an average salary of $60,000 in 2013. This might seem high by some standards but it is not enough to support the posh lifestyle. In contrast, fresh MBAs are being given $200,000 salaries immediately after graduation (Emerson, 2016).
Therefore, it is imperative to note that entrepreneurship is not for the rich and may not even lead to riches, either.
6. Entrepreneurship needs huge funding
Many people believe that for you to start a business, you must be having huge cash, and to get that cash, you have to deal and wheel with venture capitalists, angel investors, and the big people who ride around in Rolls Royce’s. In really, most of the entrepreneurial funding mostly comes from their back pocket. According to Bell (2014), most start-ups will cost approximately $25,000 to pick up but many venture capitalists mostly invest in technology and biotechnology.
It is a myth that immodesty rich investor will bestow millions of dollars in your business idea. Mainly, angel investors comprise of ordinary people who are able to make ordinary amount of money, out of which 32% live on income of at most $40,000. At such level, one can easily forget about Rolls Royce’s.
Can an entrepreneur be bankrolled? Most of the time they do not but get bootstrap.
Some entrepreneur can get lucky and be funded. Nevertheless, this is not a prerequisite for trade.
7. Entrepreneurship is fun!
This is both true and false dichotomy. Entrepreneurship is fun but truth be told, entrepreneurship is hard, and at times it can be unbearable. The challenges of entrepreneurship parallel the challenges of ordinary life. There are both good and bad times but the difference in entrepreneurship is that good times are a lot better and bad times are a lot “badder.” It is not fun all the time.

8. Entrepreneurs love huge risks
   According to our jacked-up ideology on safety, entrepreneurs are risk-takers. But maybe, the risk taken by an entrepreneur may be nothing more than just a tilt toward unconventional, dissatisfaction, and good idea with the status quo. The risks taken by an entrepreneur are not the type of devil-may-care and reckless upstart. Normally, they are decisions that are well calculated, dream-backed, and data-driven and pursued through a teeth-grinding determination.

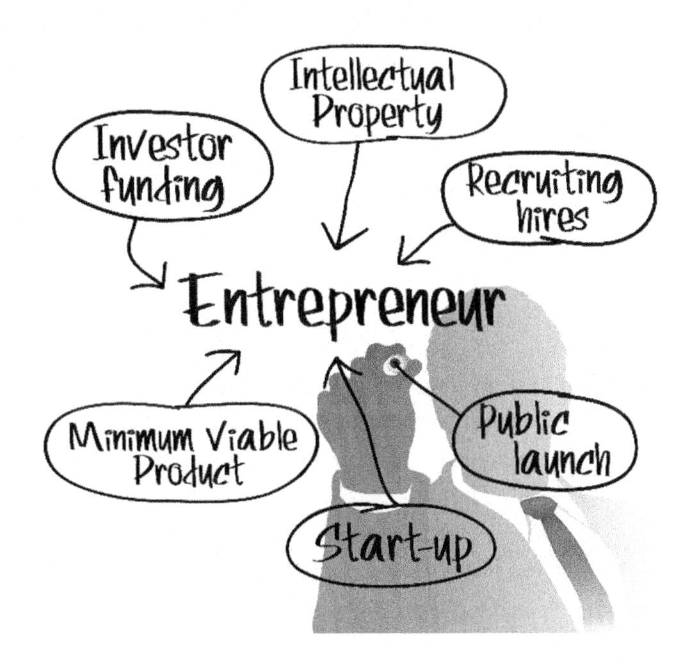


In conclusion, anyone who aspires to become an entrepreneur should shun these myths. It is an exercise in folly to classify and list characteristics, strengths, and traits of successful entrepreneurs. By their actual definition, entrepreneurs can be considered as disruptors and mold-breakers. To be successful in entrepreneurship, it is critical to first do away with all the beliefs that you have ever heard or led about entrepreneurship. On the other hand, be enthusiastic about your idea! If you are not enthusiastic about it, how can you expect others to be????

## Chapter One Questions

### Choose Either True or False

1. An entrepreneur is a person who comes up with an idea and creates a new business amidst uncertainty and risk to achieve profits and growth opportunities.
   - *True*
   - *False*

2. Entrepreneurs must in most cases make decisions in a highly uncertain environment with considerable emotional investment.
   - *True*
   - *False*
3. Typically, an entrepreneur learns from failures more than the successes.
   - *True*
   - *False*
4. The motivation to manage one's own business is usually driven out of personal profits.
   - *True*
   - *False*
5. An entrepreneur with a loss of orientation should rarely talk about the failure of the business.
   - *True*
   - *False*
6. We all need people to be employers. Therefore, we can say that business ownership is for anyone.
   - *True*
   - *False*
7. The economic theories of entrepreneurship recognize open and dynamic nature of market systems as well as taking into consideration the uniqueness of entrepreneurial activity and downplay the diverse contexts within which entrepreneurship occurs.
   - *True*
   - *False*
8. According to opportunity based theory people having strong internal control locus believe that their actions can easily influence the external world.
   - *True*
   - *False*
9. Women entrepreneur in GCC are more educated than men but have low access to employment when compared to their male counterparts.
   - *True*
   - *False*
10. Entrepreneurs are aware of what exactly they want, and know how to go for it, and they never quit.
   - *True*
   - *False*

### *Multiple Choice Questions*

11. When a person initiates a decision to start a business, several factors have to be put into consideration. Which one of the below factors is the most important?
   A. Decision-making
   B. Drafting a business plan
   C. Seeking funds
   D. Employing people to assist in doing the business

12. Which of the following is not an aspect of being an entrepreneur?
    A. Creation process
    B. Devotion of effort and time
    C. Protection of the most valuable assets
    D. Assuming the necessary risks
13. Which of the below is NOT among the questions that an entrepreneur needs to understand regarding finances before undertaking any business include the following:
    A. How attractive is the market for the new product/service?
    B. Does the business idea have the features that can attract investors?
    C. How much capital are you willing to invest?
    D. Is the business's track record clean enough to allow all forms of financial help?
14. Which of the following is NOT among the reasons why people become entrepreneurs?
    A. Opportunity
    B. Become Risk Takers
    C. Desire for Change
    D. Autonomy
15. According to psychological theories of entrepreneurship, the entrepreneurial behavior is driven by
    A. Social networks and human resources
    B. Technological, cultural, and social changes
    C. Resilience, creativity, and optimism
    D. Desire for meaningful life, social–political environment, and ethnic identification
16. Which of the following is not among the components of sociocultural environment that affect entrepreneurship?
    A. Religion
    B. Beliefs
    C. Lifestyle
    D. Political stability
17. Which is the order of steps in business setup?
    i. License and other documentation
    ii. Business TIN and bank accounts
    iii. Clearance of the name
    iv. Make a decision
    v. Business location
    vi. Decision on Joint venture, limited company or sole proprietorship
    vii. Decision on the form of business
    A. i, ii, iv, iii, v, vii, vi
    B. iv, vii, vi, iii, v, i, ii
    C. v, vii, iv, vi, ii, i, v
    D. iv, vi, vii, iii, v, i, ii

18. Which of the following is NOT among the myths of entrepreneurship?
    A. Entrepreneurs are aware of what exactly they want and know how to go for it
    B. An entrepreneur is his/her own boss
    C. Entrepreneurs should not be connected
    D. Entrepreneurship needs huge funding
19. Why is the participation of women in entrepreneurship in GCC very limited?
    A. Lack of education
    B. Sociocultural restrictions and customs
    C. Inadequate funding
    D. Political instability
20. A successful entrepreneur should be experienced in managing personal finances. Which of the following is not among the ways through which an entrepreneur can manage the finances?
    A. Planning for bad days
    B. Separating business finances from business money
    C. Diversifying in alternate investments
    D. Employing someone to manage your finances

**Note: Answers in Appendix Section.**

## References


Alalawi, A. I., & Alali, F. M. (2015). Factors affecting E-commerce adoption in SMEs in GCC: an empirical study of Kuwait. *Research Journal of Information Technology*, *7*(1), 1–21.

Al-Sadi, R., Belwal, R., & Al-Badi, R. (2013). Woman entrepreneurship in the Al-Batinah region of Oman: an identification of the barriers. *Journal of International Women's Studies*, *12*(3), 58–75.

Barreto, H. (2013). *The entrepreneur in microeconomic theory: Disappearance and explanation*. Routledge.

Barringer, B. (2012). *Entrepreneurship: Successfully launching new ventures*.

Bell, J. R. (2014). *Think like an entrepreneur*. US: Palgrave Macmillan.

Bilal, Z. O., & Al Mqbali, N. S. (2015). Challenges and constrains faced by small and medium enterprises (SMEs) in Al Batinah governorate of Oman. *World Journal of Entrepreneurship, Management and Sustainable Development*, *11*(2), 120–130.

Blank, S. (2013). Why the lean start-up changes everything. *Harvard Business Review*, *91*(5), 63–72.

Emerson, M. (2016). Your network is your net worth: building your relationship currency. In *50 billion dollar boss*. United States: Palgrave Macmillan.

Ennis, C. A. (2015). Between trend and necessity: top-down entrepreneurship promotion in Oman and Qatar. *The Muslim World*, *105*(1), 116–118.

Jayawarna, D., Jones, O., & Macpherson, A. (2015). Becoming an entrepreneur*Entrepreneurial learning. New perspectives in research, education and practice*, *4*, 20–24.

Pauceanu, A. (2016). Innovation and entrepreneurship in Sultanate of Oman – an empirical study. *Purushartha: A Journal of Management Ethics and Spirituality*.

Rice, A. L. (2013). *The enterprise and its environment: A system theory of management organization*. Routledge.

CHAPTER 2

# Small and Medium Enterprises in Oman and GCC

## Chapter Outline



## Small- and Medium-Sized Enterprises in Gulf Cooperation Council

### Introduction

Small- and medium-sized enterprises (SMEs), also known as small- and medium-sized businesses (SMBs), refer to the businesses with personnel falling below certain limits (Boohene, Ofori, Boateng, & Boohene, 2015). The definition of an SME is country-specific but are generally defined using three words: small, single, and local.

- **Small**—SMEs/SMBs are small in nature and this is based on the number of employees, capital, and assets or overall turnover.
- **Single**—Most SMEs have single owner, single service, or single product.

Entrepreneurship in the Gulf Cooperation Council.

- **Local**—Essentially, SMEs are local in nature and have a localized market. Sometimes they may be operating from the place of residence, popularly referred to as small office home office

Some of the exceptions to the aforementioned definition include the following:

- Though an SME have a small output, there is possibility of it getting a global market if it produces goods in excess.
- SMEs are not limited to any type of industry. They can be in trading, manufacturing, distribution, export and import, service company, and rental or small processing units among others.
- SMEs are legally registered hence different from other companies in informal sector.

### *Definition of Small- and Medium-Sized Enterprises in Gulf Cooperation Council*

Many private and public SMEs in the world normally base their definitions on number of employees. Contrary, the SMEs in Gulf Cooperation Council (GCC) do not have a standardized way of defining SME. The definition is based on the number of employees, annual turnover, and the assets in the company.

### *Small- and Medium-Sized Enterprises Definition in Oman (Table 2.1)*

The Supreme Council for Planning in Oman defines SMEs as the following:

- Microenterprises as having up to 5 employees
- Small enterprises as having up to 20 employees
- Medium enterprises as having up to 100 employees

### *Current Trends of Small- and Medium-Sized Enterprises in Gulf Cooperation Council*

SMEs in GCC have had difficulties to access funding from commercial banks. Some of the drawbacks of the traditional funding methods include extensive and time-consuming

**Table 2.1: Small- and Medium-Sized Enterprises Classification in Sultanate of Oman (Source: Public Authority for Small and Medium Enterprises Development)**

| Category | Number of Employees | Financial Revenue (OR) |
|---|---|---|
| Micro corporation | 1 until 5 | Less than 100,000 |
| Small corporation | 6 until 25 | 100,000–500,000 |
| Medium corporation | 26 until 99 | 500,000–3,000,000 |

documentation, high interest rates, very high fines of late or early repayments, and short repayment periods (Baldwin, 2012). Such challenges have compelled many economically advanced countries to develop alternative funding methods to balance between protection of borrowing regulations and motivating the entrepreneurial spirit. Some of the alternative forms of funding include venture capital, private equity companies, and equity from angel investors (Al-Mubaraki & Busler, 2011).

The GCC has started experiencing innovative funding methods. For instance, an agency in Qatar mandated with development of SMEs sector in the region has formulated the equity investment initiative that is aimed at increasing the amount of capital ejected to the SME sector. This is achievable through participation of venture capitalists, private equity companies, and angel investors (Mishra, Rabi, Rath, & Al Yahai, 2014). Also, the agency is mandated with preparation of the domestic directory for angel equity investors solely dedicated to SMEs. Other similar initiatives have also been adopted from which the GCC can use by customizing and implementing them. These include InnovFin from European Union, which allows noninstitutionalized participation from India to necessitate the investment of SMEs in stock exchanges, as well as allow banks within the public sector issue promissory stocks to the SMEs in the region (Rietveld & Bruinsma, 2012).

The efforts by the GCC in encouraging the private equity within the SME sector may experience several challenges. For instance, investors might be more interested in companies within the digital sector- or tech-based companies. This may affect SMEs that are not tech-based which experience similar capital problems such as manufacturing. To mitigate this challenge, the governments within the GCC should develop policies that assist SMEs that are unable to attract the private equity investors (Ismail, 2014). This can be achieved through employment of the "funds-of-funds" where government invests in venture capital rather than investing directly in SMEs. The capital should in return identify viable financing opportunities.

The presence of crowd funding is accessible to SMEs within GCC where funds are raised from single or multiple entities mostly through Internet and the funds channeled toward a common investment (Rice, 2013). Such a concept started with Aflamnah, which was the first UAE-based crowd funding that allows people from GCC to raise money to finance ideas in untapped areas such as television, art, and music (Fernandez & Ali, 2014). Also, the SMEs from GCC region have adopted the peer-to-peer lending that enhances the access to capital at a low interest rate with minimal penalty risks. This can be beneficial in development of business during the early development phases. Proper management structures are critical in strengthening Islamic financing options since they enhance protection and address the concerns and rights of lenders. This also plays a major role in increasing the confidence of the banks in lending (Yalcin, 2014).

### *Importance of Small- and Medium-Sized Enterprises in Gulf Cooperation Council*

SMEs have been beneficial to GCC in the following ways:

- SMEs have contributed significantly, everywhere, to growth and development of efficiency, especially to job creation, innovativeness, and increased international competitiveness. They can, therefore, be considered as the main drivers for economic growth and diversification.
- SMEs act as the backbone for any long-term sustainable and successful economy. They act as blood cells for the any successfully diversified large corporations and economies. The best example in this case is Switzerland's economy, where more than 75% of economy income is generated from SMEs' activities.
- SMEs provide local jobs due to their local roots but can also exploit the globalization opportunities. It is worthy to mention here, as example, the major contribution of Raysut Industrial Estate, Salalah Port, and Salalah Free Zone, which offer priority to local SMEs in their acquisition process.
- Job creation and economic diversification for Gulf nationals are starting to have a major impact as the development of SMEs is highly a governments' priority.

### *Contribution of Small- and Medium-Sized Enterprises to the Economy*

SMEs have been the medium for economic growth and major drivers of industrial development. Due to the sheer nature of SMEs in terms of size, operations, and numbers, their role in promoting endogenous sources of development and strengthening of the infrastructure has been recognized. SMEs have contributed to the GCC in the following ways:

1. Economic activity
   - SMEs contribute to over 40% of the merchandise export in GCC attributable to the increased number of new entrants.
   - According to the census in GCC, SMEs contribute about 50% of the total employment.
   - Service industry forms the bulk of industries in GCC's SMEs.
2. Number of firms
   - SMEs account for 99.9% of 27 million nonemployer and employers in GCC.
   - Most SMEs have less than 20 employees.
3. Employment
   - SMEs use approximately 50% of the total employment in GCC.
   - Employment in SMEs has been growing at a higher rate than in large firms and has been largely contributed by employment growth in construction and service sectors.
   - Another aspect to be considered is *tasattur* (or often called hidden trade), when the rightful owner is an expat and use a local as front for the business; it has considerable effects, both positive and negative, on the economy and the community.

4. Innovation
   - SMEs provide an important avenue for innovation, products, services, and processes more than the large firms.
5. Entrepreneurial opportunities
   - SME provides opportunities for the citizens to grow and develop their entrepreneurial skills.
   - The promotion of the domestic-centered growth in emerging and existing industries as well as strengthening of the economy resilience in a challenging and competitive environment by the SMEs is inarguable.
   - The growth in SMEs can be assessed by evaluating the contribution to agriculture, manufacturing, services, and especially tourism industry.

### *Reasons Why the Support for Small- and Medium-Sized Enterprises in Gulf Region Is Different*

SMEs in GCC are totally different from SMEs in any other part of the world (Table 2.2). This is majorly because of their extensive application of expatriate workers with very few nationals.

This is clearly shown in the labor statistics presented further for the three major players in GCC.

The labor force in private sector is majorly made of expatriate. This ranges from 76% to 96% with Qatar and UAE having the highest number of expatriates (94% and 96%), while Oman having the lowest percentage (76%).

The low-skill microenterprises are having their workforce made up of entirely expatriates. This is majorly in many laundries, barbershops, and other small business in side streets and city alleys of the Gulf region. Such an economic structure has been as a result of the formulation of policies on open labor admission and the generous compensation within the public sector. As a result, for every 10 jobs created within the private sector, at least eight goes to the

**Table 2.2: Labor Force in the Private Sector, November 2015**

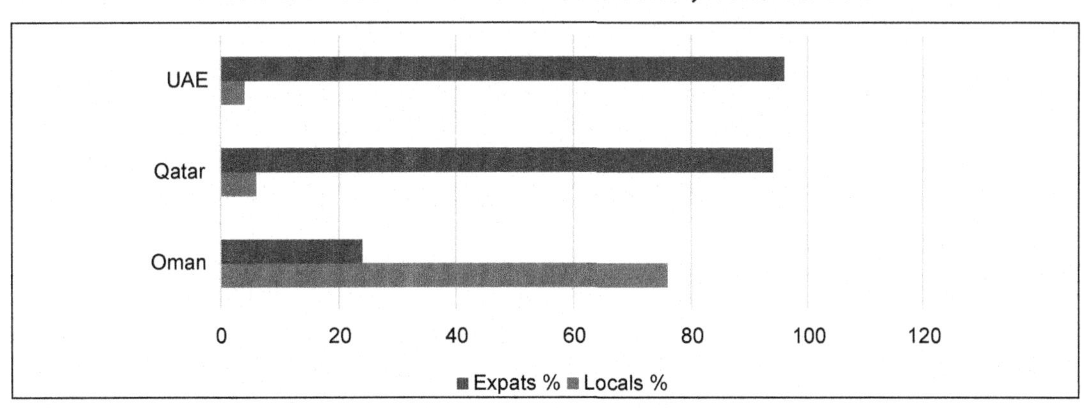


*Source: Compiled by author from collected data.*

expatriates. Meanwhile, the nationals continue gravitating toward the public sector due to attractive wages, long-term job security, and improved working conditions. The matter becomes more complicated since at other times, even the rightful when the rightful owner of the business is an expatriate and the nationals serve as front person for legal purposes, popularly referred as *tasattur (or hidden trade)*.

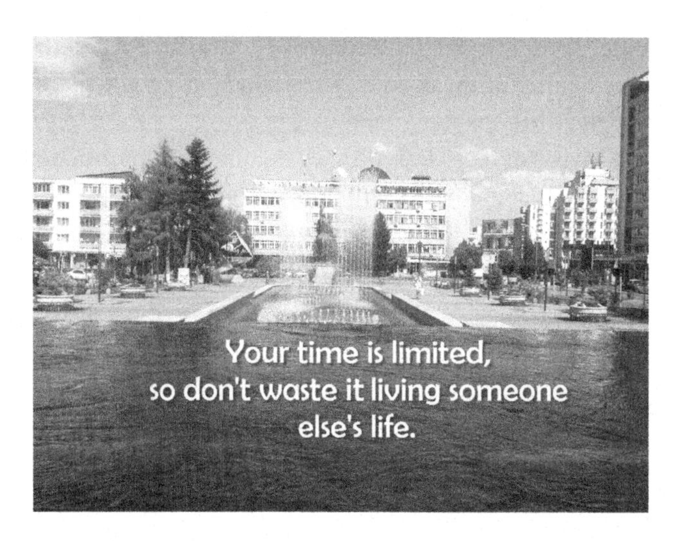


As a result, most commercial banks in the GCC area have been reluctant to fund SMEs. This is clearly shown by the reduced number of SME loans when compared to other countries. For instance, the SME loans in OECD countries totaled to 26% but 2% in GCC in 2015 (Alalawi & Alali, 2015). Banks in GCC face different challenges when compared with their counterparts in other areas. These include poor collateral, weakness in business planning among the applicants and nonexistent or informal accounts. This among many other challenges makes the banks unsure about the true ownership of the projects that are to be serviced using the requested loans.

### *Therefore, What Is a Good Small- and Medium-Sized Enterprise Support Strategy in Gulf Cooperation Council Context?*

First, rather than seeking for job creation for nationals, which is almost impossible with current GCC labor market policies, the government should promote entrepreneurship for the nationals. This implies that the main focus will be on the business potential of the person rather than on financing needs of the applicant.

- The support package should incorporate mandatory pretraining as well as in-place advisory services that will play a major role in removing the *tasattur* applicants.
- Financing should be restricted to activities that are high valued like projects that relate to information on engineering, renewable energy, and technology. While these may lead to

fewer job opportunities than the low productivity alternatives, they have high likelihood of appealing to the skilled nationals.

- Equity may be the preferred funding instruments than banks in GCC and governments should support them through financing and provision of incubation opportunities and trainings for aspiring entrepreneurs.

## Small- and Medium-Sized Enterprises in Oman

As per the records of Public Authority for SME Development, in Sultanate of Oman are registered 18.597 SMEs (December 2015), meanwhile in Dhofar Governorate we can count 1074 SMEs (Fig. 2.1). For 2016, it estimates a growth of SMEs number in Sultanate with approximately 10%. It is also worthy to mention that Al Raffd Fund (fund which offers loans for a time period of 15 years for a maximum amount of 100,000 Omani Rials), in its 2 years of activity, offered loans to 1668 persons in Sultanate of Oman, meanwhile only in Dhofar Governorate loans were granted to 208 persons (the value of the loans granted in Dhofar Governorate is approximately 9 million Rials).

SMEs constitute more than 90% of the total companies in Oman (Al-Sadi, Belwal, & Al-Badi, 2013). The prospect of the main role played by SME sector in Oman and its potential to increase the economic value was first outlined in Royal Decree 19/2007 and promulgated in March 2007. This saw the establishment of Directorate General of the Development of Small and Medium Enterprises under the Ministry of Industry and Commerce. The Directorate outlined the role of Ministry of Commerce in creating and enhancing the private sector to positively develop the Omani economy by ensuring the environment to conduct business was favorable (Ismail, 2014). The acknowledgment of the role of SMEs in development of

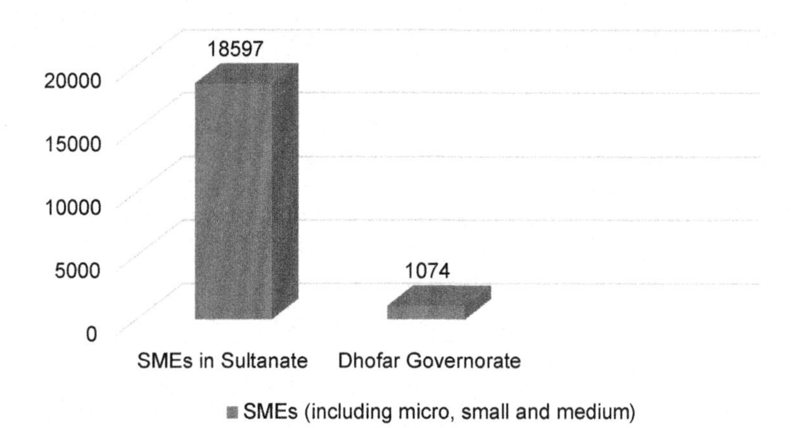


**Figure 2.1**
Small- and medium-sized enterprises in Sultanate of Oman as per December 2015.
*Source: Compiled by author.*

Sultanate as well as establishment of an institution to support the sector was a very critical and important move. Further, the *Public Authority for SMEs development* indicated further the importance of SMEs and its ultimate success was to gradually and effectively help the sector make major contribution to the Omani economy. Failure to meet these SME objectives would have rendered the institution into another level of bureaucracy and burden the public finances.

### Case Study: A Small Business Enterprise in Salalah—Sadim Business Consulting

The CEO of Sadim Business Consulting, Mr. Salim Ali Al Jabri, told us that he started the consultancy business, together with his partner, to fulfill a stringent demand from the local market. The vision of the company is "Together to achieve excellence" meanwhile the mission is to become the biggest consultancy partner in the Middle East.

"Starting from being completely unknown, we reached to serve clients all over the Sultanate, even large corporations, that found in us a reliable long-term partner. We deliver superior results to the business community while giving back to the community in which we live and work" says Mr. Salim Ali Al Jabri.

Before starting the business, Mr. Salim Ali Al Jabri had a well-written business plan, which contributed significantly to his success, along with his business partners' hard work and knowledge. The core values of the company are pursuit of excellence, transparency, integrity, collaboration, accountability, passion, and professionalism. In Mr. Salim's vision, the human resource is the most valuable resource of the business. These combined values contribute to company's success.

The today challenges in the economy worldwide determine organizational need to adapt, adjust, innovate, and try to survive. These types of challenges must be handled in creative and innovative manner. To achieve this specific purpose, the strategic vision and its communication to all interested parties are vital. There is also a shift in the business sector, some businesses are closing, others making losses while others are enlarging their business markets and making profits. The difference between these companies is their approaches and their preparedness to embrace innovation.

Mr. Salim Ali Al Jabri has faced bureaucracy, lengthy decisional process, and getting financing for the business. He did not give up and pursued his dream to see this company growing and on the path to success. Still there are many challenges to be faced and a long ride ahead, but Mr. Salim Ali Al Jabri is confident that he will achieve his dream. "We strongly believe that facts and results speaks for themselves," believes Mr. Salim.

To enter on the market and handle the challenges, the team came up with custom-made solutions, taking into consideration local specificities, all ground economic and social realities and factors involved. Nowadays, they have several companies who can testify about the quality of the service, results, and professionalism.

Sadim Business Consulting approach in regarding to advertising is mostly "word-of-mouth"; their satisfied customers recommend them to their partners who are facing challenges and need support.

"Our business is a mixture of challenges, hard work, professionalism, long hours, creativity, passion and permanent communication with all our stakeholders" finishes the discussion Mr. Salim Ali Al Jabri.

### Have Small- and Medium-Sized Enterprises Contributed to the Omani Economy?

The available statistics on SMEs in Oman indicates that the sector is yet to grow and realize the potential contribution it has to the economy.

- The Oxford Business Group report (2016) indicates that the SME sector in Oman is equivalent to 16% of the total GDP and represents 90% of the economic activities.
- Loopholes have been available in the current system in Oman where locals register as business owners while in the real sense, they are agents of expatriates and this contributes to the rent-seeking behavior by some Omani and results to economic and financial ramifications like pressure in labor markets for the Omani nationals and increased remittances. This results when destructive behaviors by large entities are removed or curtailed (Ashrafi, Sharma, Al-Badi, & Al-Gharbi, 2014).

### What Are the Roles of the Government in Saving Omani Small- and Medium-Sized Enterprise?

- The government should be in the front to mitigate the market failures as well as eliminate policy biases. All the market failures that result in low cost disadvantages for the SMEs should be eliminated.
- Government should ameliorate the transactional efficiency that relates to product, input, and financial markets relevant to SMEs by enhancing easy access to information. There is also need to develop mechanisms that manage the risks in SMEs.
- The World Bank study have been emphasizing on importance of reconsidering public policy as well as that regulations that perpetuate discrimination against SMEs (D'Angelo, Majocchi, & Buck, 2016). The policies should also be critical in promoting entrepreneurship, improve the accessibility to venture capital as well as facilitate the start-up and expansion of firms (Schwalje, 2013). Given tables present the ranking of Oman's economy by World Bank on the ease of doing business (Fig. 2.2) and the time taken to get the company ready for start-up.
- The promotion of development of the secondary stock markets can lessen the burden on taxes for dividends and capital gains to allow use of more stock options in compensating the smaller firms.
- Promotion of networks between the owners and investors of SMEs may be critical in bridging the information gap, hence promote cooperation.

**Challenges Facing Small- and Medium-Sized Enterprises in Sultanate of Oman**

According to a senior commercial bank official in Oman, the Central Bank of Oman (CBO) can play a major role in enhancing the existing procedures as far as lending to SMEs is concerned. The current procedures prompt the banks to classify the business loans as nonpaid in case the business fails to service that loan within 90 days. This compels many banks to report and take nonpayment cases to courts to recover the amount lent since many of the loans involved backing by collaterals such as retirement wages, business itself, or even land. Due to the increased challenges facing SMEs, there is a great need to extend the loan repayment to 180 days. The failure to meet the regular repayments to banks is because even the most successful SMEs experience challenges in their cash flows. For instance, the enterprises may be providing products and/or services to large companies or government entities, which in most cases take time to honor their payments on time. Such challenges translate into cash flow problems and by default affect the regular loan repayments to the banks. To mitigate such challenges, the government should establish the fast track systems while at the same time encouraging large companies to follow their steps. The Public Authority for Development of SMEs should include the average period of repayments to the SMEs in their annual reports. This would act as an incentive for big business in their expedition of payments to SMEs. The performance on progress made in shortening the time required for the repayments could thereafter be used as an indicator in supporting SMEs. The tenders awarded to the SMEs should outline the repayment and expedition terms for SMEs as priority (Ennis, 2015).

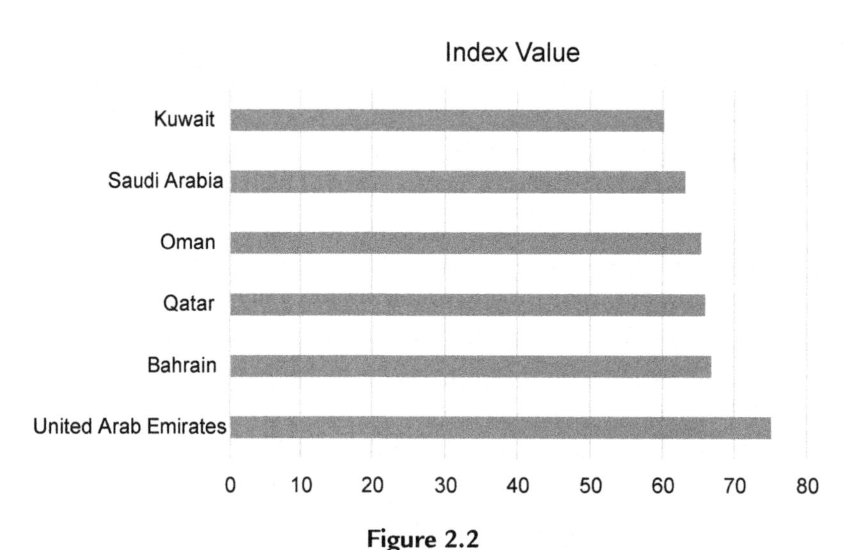


**Figure 2.2**
Ease of doing Business in Gulf Cooperation Council, 2016. *Adapted after Pauceanu, A.M. (2016). Foreign investment promotion analysis in Sultanate of Oman: the case of Dhofar Governorate.* International Journal of Economics and Financial Issues, 6*(2), 392–401.*

The SMEs in Oman have been facing problems when conducting professional feasibility studies as well as the inadequate collaterals required to retrieve line of credit.

Most of the incentives such as those offered by the economic zones (also called free zones) meant to assist the nationals in starting or growing their businesses are currently being channeled to expatriates. Such a reality of hidden economy affects the foreign direct investment policy by the government to promote an upward entrepreneurship and mobility through starting a business venture or expanding the existing one (Alalawi & Alali, 2015).

These challenges have left the Oman Development Bank (ODB) as the main SME lender. The business model used by ODB depends on low cost funding or government equity and large interest rate subsidies on long-term loans. The prevalence of the low interest rates by the ODB plays a major role in crowding out the long-term lending from commercial banks to SMEs. At basic level, the sector has been confronting challenges in marketing, technical, administrative, regulatory, and organizational limitations (Yalcin, 2014).

For the SMEs to thrive in Oman and achieve the potential social and economic benefits, the owners should be fully engaged in start-ups as well as in all the growth phases of the business.

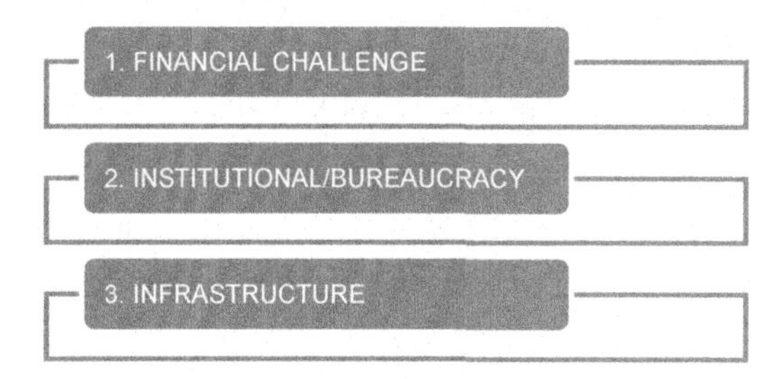


The challenges experienced by SMEs in Oman can be classified into three categories: financial, institutional, and infrastructure.

The institutional, financial, and infrastructure challenges affect both the demand and supply side of the SME sector.

- A study by World Bank portrayed institutional constraints include the incentive gaps for the young Omani nationals to work in large private companies or outside public sector, labor regulations, poor business skills, and excess bureaucracy to obtain business and work permits.
- The financial challenges include those challenges experienced on both the supply and demand side that limit any lending to SMEs. For instance, limited competition among

banks and high margins affect the supply side as results in very little incentives to fund SMEs. On demand side, banks have few viable projects.
- In terms of infrastructure, there is still little support for SMEs, like appropriate support services, professional networking, redundant electrical power supply, inflexible lease terms, or lack of mentors.

### *Growth Opportunity for the Small- and Medium-Sized Enterprise in Oman*

The SMEs sector in Oman is relatively underdeveloped but provides a significant potential. The outlays of the discretionary spending in terms of capital expenditure for the infrastructural projects present a significant opportunity for SME sector's accessibility to supply. Also, the foreign direct investment policy and investment policy in Sultanate will make SMEs as part of overall industrial policy to promote links as well as transfer knowledge from large to smaller companies (Pauceanu, 2016) The policy-makers have, as part of overall strategy, identified the logistic and transport sector as a major area that will enhance future growth in Oman, especially due to the proximity of the country to Indian Ocean. Among the major industries that will see a turnaround of the Omani economy is health care, manufacturing, logistics, and tourism (Darwish, 2014).

Due to the variety and magnitude of the investments expected in Oman, there is a great need to formulate a strategy map that will help in identifying the synergies between the projects within the Omani SME sector. The road map and strategy should include both the pre- and postimplementation opportunities for the SME sector (Bilal & Al Mqbali, 2015).

There is a new trend among the GCC companies that are owned by GCC citizens: this trend refers to have a supply-oriented policy, which gives priority to local SMEs and their products and services. The author estimates that if this trend will continue and increase, the GCC is having a chance to a long-term sustainable economy and further development. GCC companies needs visionary leaders, which can contribute to this goal.

**Case Study: Omani Woman Entrepreneur**

Etab Al Zadjali together with four other women started the Cake Gallery in 2010. Currently, they have a team of 50 employees and 6 outlets in various areas in Oman. From the event that was held at one of the outlets in Mawaleh in the presence of entrepreneurs from Sultanate was aimed at assisting and empowering entrepreneurs on the power of unleashing new ideas.

Driven by passion, Etab has grown loving sweets, a factor that has contributed to her translation into a fruitful business.

According to her, she has, just like any other business, experienced good and bad times for her to reach where she is currently. "Significant efforts were undertaken till this project was able to see success. When I first started business, my aspiration was to contribute with a precious project for Oman," Etab said, adding: "Cake Gallery's success is certainly attributed to the dedication and commitment of its team. Besides, competitors are always there, yet I always hunt for distinction in what I do through what I offer to the customers to make them happily satisfied."

Etab has been supported by the AL Balushi Investment LLC, especially in management.

Etab has always translated her passions to real business opportunity. Her passion for the kids' projects saw her starting birthday preparations as well as offering halls for birthday parties. Additionally, Etab operates a ladies' salon.

Malak Al Shaibani, the manager of a local bank, has all along emphasized that women should be in the forefront to make changes in the society as they represent almost half of the society. This triggered the start-up of Najihat programme that is normally organized with the support of National Bank of Oman. The relationship manager, Asila Al Obaidani, in National Bank of Oman has emphasized the need to support SMEs. "Since the National Bank of Oman pays a great attention to the SMEs in Oman, we are privileged to be supporting NBC's Najihat initiative," Asila commented.

This bank has been offering a generous banking offer for the SMEs across Sultanate. In addition to the offering extensive network of branches, it has been providing SMEs with the best corporate banking portal for conducting their business transactions easily from the comfort of their offices. The bank has collaborated with Najihat programme to bring four sessions in every 3 months where women meet in the location of the business owner who shares the fruitful experience and start-up challenges. The series of the programme has been inspiring Omani women and prospective entrepreneurs to start up their own business ventures.

Such an event presents the people with innovative ideas and supports those who are passionate about entering into entrepreneurship pitch. Other similar events include National Business Center that is an initiative of public establishment for industrial estates and aims at offering a platform to the promising Omani entrepreneurs to develop and advance their ideas to growing and profitable ventures. The center has also been instrumental in providing support, trainings, mentoring, guidance, and access to industry experts and markets (Al-Sadi et al., 2013).

## Chapter Two Questions

### Choose Either True or False

1. Definition of SME varies from one country to another.
   - *True*
   - *False*
2. Bank loans are the best and easily accessible form of funding for SMEs.
   - *True*
   - *False*

3. Peer-to-peer lending has been adopted in GCC to facilitate the accessibility to capital, which is beneficial in development of business during the early development phases.
   - *True*
   - *False*
4. SMEs in GCC are very similar to SMEs in other parts of the world.
   - *True*
   - *False*
5. SMEs contribute to over 40% of the merchandise export in GCC attributable to the increased number of new entrants.
   - *True*
   - *False*
6. Labor force in Oman is mainly made up of expatriates.
   - *True*
   - *False*
7. The statistics available on SMEs in Oman shows that the sector has realized its peak growth and has contributed greatly to the Omani economy.
   - *True*
   - *False*
8. Logistics and transport are the main sectors that will play a major role in development of SME sector especially because of proximity to Indian Ocean.
   - *True*
   - *False*
9. There should be a well-outlined road map and strategy toward identification of synergies between the projects within the Omani SME sector due to the variety and magnitude of the investments expected in Oman.
   - *True*
   - *False*
10. The prevalence of the low interest rates by the Oman Development Bank is ineffective when crowding out the long-term lending from commercial banks to SMEs.
   - *True*
   - *False*

### *Multiple Choice Questions*

11. The definition of SME varies from country to country. However, the definition should incorporate three key words. Which one of the key words given is NOT used in defining SME?
   A. Single
   B. Local
   C. Profitable
   D. Small

12. Which one of the following is a definition of SME by Ministry of National Economy in Oman?
    A. Microenterprises as having up to 10 employees
    B. Small enterprises as having up to 15 employees
    C. Medium enterprises as having up to 100 employees
    D. Medium-sized companies with up to 100 workers
13. Which of the given types of funding is not an alternative funding method for SMEs in GCC region?
    A. Venture capital
    B. Bank loans
    C. Private equity companies
    D. Equity from angel investors
14. The effort to encourage private equity within the SME sector in GCC is likely to experience one of the given challenges. Which one is it?
    A. Increased interests by potential investors in tech-based or digital ventures
    B. Reduced intervention from the government
    C. Lack of foreign direct investments
    D. Poor structural frameworks of the SME
15. Which one of the following is not a contribution of SME to the Omani economy?
    A. Economic Activity
    B. Reduction in exports
    C. Employment
    D. Innovation
16. Why are many banks in GCC reluctant to give loans to SMEs?
    A. Poor structural framework of SMEs
    B. Inadequate disposable funds to loan out to SMEs
    C. Fear of failure of SMEs
    D. Poor legal ownership of local businesses due to increased entry of expatriates
17. A good SME support strategy in GCC should include all of the following except one. Which is it?
    A. Should incorporate mandatory training and in-place advisory services
    B. Strict financing on high-valued projects
    C. Introduction of equity funding rather than bank funding
    D. Chasing away the expatriates
18. Which of the following is a main loophole in SMEs system in Oman?
    A. Omani locals register as business owners but are agents of expatriates
    B. Lack of government support
    C. Inaccessibility to adequate funding
    D. Poor local markets

19. Given list presents the different categories of challenges experienced by SMEs in Oman. Which one is NOT among the three categories?
    A. Institution
    B. Financial
    C. Social
    D. Infrastructural
20. Which of the following shows how SMEs have contributed to the economy in GCC?
    A. Contributes to the growth in country's GDP
    B. Increased employment opportunities for the locals
    C. A and B
    D. None of the above

**Note: Answers in Appendix Section.**

## References


Alalawi, A. I., & Alali, F. M. (2015). Factors affecting E-commerce adoption in SMEs in GCC: an empirical study of Kuwait. *Research Journal of Information Technology*, *7*(1), 1–21.

Al-Mubaraki, H., & Busler, M. (2011). The incubators economic indicators: mixed approaches. *Journal of Case Research in Business and Economics*, 1–12.

Al-Sadi, R., Belwal, R., & Al-Badi, R. (2013). Woman entrepreneurship in the Al-Batinah region of Oman: an identification of the barriers. *Journal of International Women's Studies*, *12*(3), 58–75.

Ashrafi, R., Sharma, S. K., Al-Badi, A. H., & Al-Gharbi, K. (2014). Achieving business success through information and communication technologies adoption by small and medium enterprises in Oman. *Middle-East Journal of Scientific Research*, *22*(1), 138–146.

Baldwin, C. Y. (2012). Organization design for business ecosystems. *Journal of Organization Design*, *1*(1), 34–37.

Bilal, Z. O., & Al Mqbali, N. S. (2015). Challenges and constrains faced by small and medium enterprises (SMEs) in Al Batinah governorate of Oman. *World Journal of Entrepreneurship, Management and Sustainable Development*, *11*(2), 120–130.

Boohene, R., Ofori, D., Boateng, B. D., & Boohene, K. A. (2015). Information and communication technology usage and small and medium-sized enterprises growth in the Accra Metropolis. *Journal of Business and Enterprise Development*, *5*(1), 101–110.

D'Angelo, A., Majocchi, A., & Buck, T. (2016). External managers, family ownership and the scope of SME internationalization. *Journal of World Business*, 12–17.

Darwish, S. (2014). The role of universities in developing small and medium enterprises (SMEs): future challenges for Oman. *International Business and Management*, *8*(2), 70–77.

Ennis, C. A. (2015). Between trend and necessity: top-down entrepreneurship promotion in Oman and Qatar. *The Muslim World*, *105*(1), 116–118.

Fernandez, R. K., & Ali, S. (2014). *SME contribution for diversification and stability in emerging economies.*

Ismail, S. (2014). Critical success factors for TQM implementation and their impact on performance of SMEs. *International journal of productivity and performance management*, *58*(3), 215–237.

Mishra, D., Rabi, N., Rath, D. P., & Al Yahai, Q. (2014). *Concentration and competition in Oman's banking sector implications for financial stability.*

Pauceanu, A. M. (2016). Foreign investment promotion analysis in Sultanate of Oman: the case of Dhofar Governorate. *International Journal of Economics and Financial Issues*, *6*(2), 392–401.

Rice, A. L. (2013). *The enterprise and its environment: A system theory of management organization.* Routledge.

Rietveld, P., & Bruinsma, F. (2012). *Is transport infrastructure effective? Transport infrastructure and accessibility: impacts on the space economy*. Heidelberg: Springer Science & Business Media.

Schwalje, W. (2013). *A conceptual model of national skills formation for knowledge-based economic development in the Arab world* Available at SSRN 1809205.

Yalcin, S. (2014). SMEs: their role in developing growth and the potential for investors. *CFA Institute Conference Proceedings Quarterly*, *31*(3), 7–11.

CHAPTER 3

# Business Feasibility Study

## Chapter Outline



## Introduction

A feasibility study is the exploration of viability of an idea (Glackin, 2013). The study provides answer on whether or not to proceed with the idea proposed. All the activities of a feasibility study are geared toward answering the question, "Should we proceed with the project idea proposed?"

Feasibility studies are used in different ways but the primary objective is on proposed business ventures. An entrepreneur should conduct a feasibility study to determine how viable the business idea is before proceeding with business development (Tito & Anderson, 2013). Early determination of a workable business idea saves money, later heartache and time. It helps flush out a business idea and determine if investment into the business idea is warranted. In simple terms, a feasibility study can be considered as an assessment that provides a platform on which a "go" or a "no-go" decision is reached. While a feasibility study acts as a vetting process to give a prospective entrepreneur a realistic view of the business, a business plan provides a road map of the business for 3–5 years. A feasible venture refers to the business activity that will generate enough profits and cash flow for the business as well as withstanding the risks encountered and remains viable so as to meet the objectives of the founders (Ghisi & Schondermark, 2013).

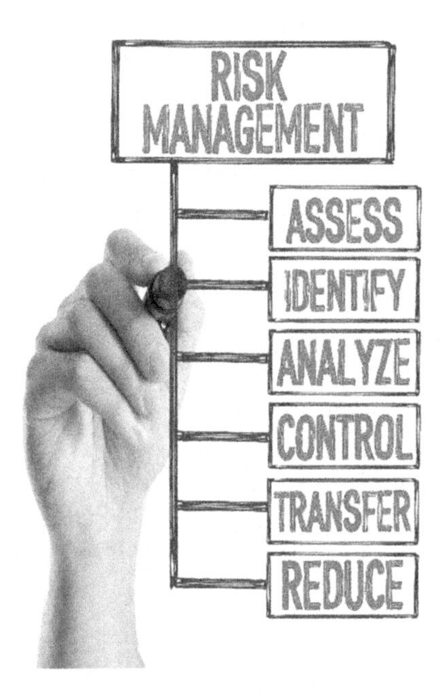

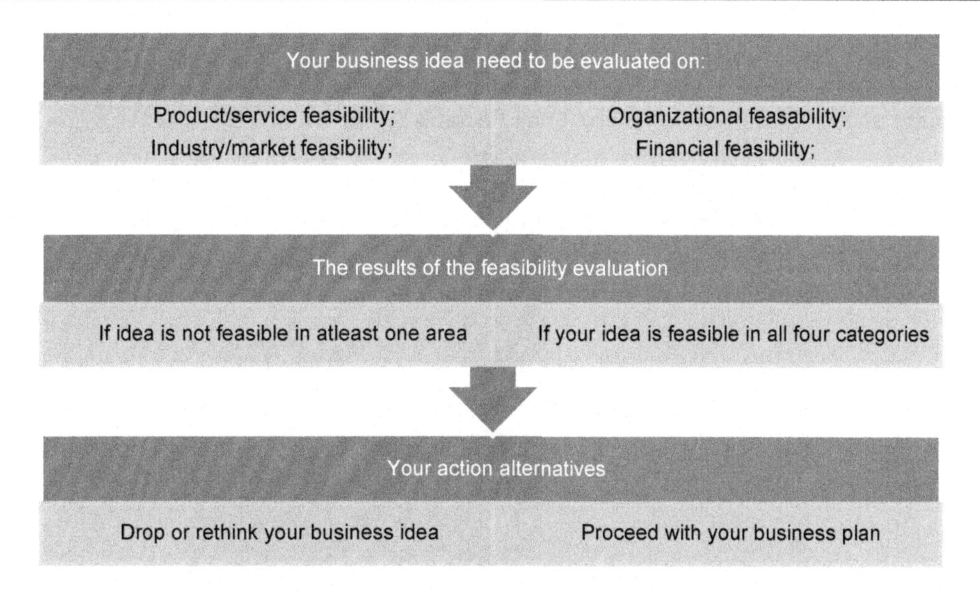


**Figure 3.1**
Evaluation of the business idea. *Adapted after Barreto, H. (2013).* The entrepreneur in microeconomic theory: Disappearance and explanation. *Routledge.*

Feasibility analysis entails the preliminary evaluation of an idea to determine whether or not to pursue the idea. The analysis takes the guesswork out of business launch and allows the entrepreneur a more secure notion of the idea being more viable or secure. Any business idea that is determined to be unworkable should be rethought or dropped. When exposed to a rethought, a slightly different version of the idea emerges, which in any way should be exposed to a similar level of feasibility study as the original idea. The pattern of feasibility study is represented in Fig. 3.1.

Many entrepreneurs never follow this pattern before they are launching of a venture. Surveys conducted by Goel and Karri (2006) show that many entrepreneurs will underestimate their competition in the marketplace and overestimate their chances for success.

When the idea is deemed feasible, a lot of work should be done to flesh out the idea completely before writing the business plan and launching the venture. When the feasibility analysis is positive, an entrepreneur gets the green light on how to pursue the idea further. Every component of the feasibility analysis should be explored completely in preparation for launching the venture (Barringer, 2012).

For instance, a business idea that was developed by **Trakus Inc.** gives a perfect example of the importance of feasibility study. Unlike **Iridium**, the Trakus Inc. has used feasibility analysis in a very effective manner so as to determine the viability of the idea before spending time and effort on it. This is illustrated further.

**Feasibility of Satellite Phones: Were They Feasible?**

When Bertinger's wife, an engineer in Motorola, failed to reach her customers through cell phone after she went for vacation in Caribbean, she came up with an idea. She thought that if a constellation of 66 low-orbiting satellites was placed in space, the subscribers would be in a position to make calls from any place on earth. This was not a very new idea. There were satellite phones already but during this time, there were challenges with the satellite phones. The phones could only be used at high altitudes and were very heavy with a quarter of a second delay in voice. She envisioned that use of low altitude satellites could have resulted to phones that were smaller in size with an imperceptible voice delay. She referred to this idea as Iridium. This looked like a perfect idea. Nevertheless, it was not exposed to feasibility analysis and found not to be viable. Following are the reasons:

First, to build satellites and fix them in orbit, the Motorola company established a separate company, Iridium LLC, in 1991. The related costs were enormous. This exposed the company to very huge debts. In November 1998, the company launched the service. This was characterized by the vice president, Al Gore, making the first call using the technology. The charges were $3000 for a phone while the calls were charged between $3 and $8 per minute. From the initial stages, Iridium was aware that the phone would have been very big and the services would have been too costly to compete with the traditional phones. Its target market was, therefore, people who traveled frequently in areas where the cellular services were unavailable. These included construction workers in remote regions, international business travelers, military forces, off-shore oil rig employees, and workers in deep sea ships. The executive chief by then, Edward Staiano, predicted that the company would be having over 500,000 subscribers by the end of 1999. However, by July 1999, Iridium had only 20,000 subscribers and needed extra 52,000 subscribers to meet the loan obligations. By August 1999, Iridium defaulted over $1.5 billion in loans after which it was filed for bankruptcy.

**Feasibility of Satellite Phones: Were They Feasible?—cont'd**

**What Went Wrong?**

Many things went wrong. First, due to the level of complexity of the technology, Iridium concept took 11 years to be developed fully and at the same time, the traditional cell phone service was spreading at a much high rate than Iridium's anticipation. By the time Iridium was launched and made available to users, good share of the previously determined target market could have met its needs through the traditional cell phones that were lighter and cheaper and were working effectively in many areas.

Second, since the technology was dependent on line of sight between the orbiting satellite and the antenna of the phone, the functionality of the phone remained limited. This implied that it could not have been used inside the buildings, in moving cars and in many urban areas where the tall buildings easily obstructed the line of sight between the satellite and the phone.

A book by Sydney Finkelstein, a professor at Dartmouth College, on "Why Smart Executives Fail" shows that in his study of failure of Iridium, a top consultant had told him that "You can't expect a CEO traveling on business in Bangkok to leave a building, walk outside to a street corner, and pull out a $3000 phone." For instance, in remote areas, the battery needed customized solar-powered accessories, hence unappealing to busiest travelers.

It was very unfortunate that there was no effective feasibility analysis that Iridium engaged in prior to spending billion dollars for the idea to spectacularly fail. Professor Finkelstein quotes the second CEO of Iridium, John Richardson, "We're a classic MBA case study in how not to introduce a product. First we created a marvelous technological achievement. Then we asked how to make money on it."

Continued

**Feasibility of Satellite Phones: Were They Feasible?—cont'd**

One is left to ask why the leaders of Iridium continued pushing for the concept despite the challenges encountered during the early stages. Would it have been cheaper to plug out the venture sooner than it actually happened? Among some of the problems Iridium experienced was the advancing technologies in cell phone industry. As an entrepreneur, what is the best method that one should adopt to remain ahead of technological developments? What can you do to monitor the meaning of technological advancement to the success of your business? Why did Iridium financial backers and founders failed to conduct a more thorough feasibility study beforehand? What can a start-up entrepreneur learn from the experience of Iridium on importance of feasibility study? (*Source: Pip Coburn, New York: Penguin Group.*)

On the other hand, **Trakus company**, previously known as **Retailing Insights**, was founded in 1997. The main business idea was to come up with computerized shopping carts for the grocery stores referred to as video carts. The carts were to use wireless technology to give notifications on whereabouts of each cart in the store as well as provide other useful information that was to be displayed on a video attached to the cart. For instance, a shopper in cereal aisle would have the cart having the adverts for cereals and help the shopper know the brands that are on sale. Also, the video carts were to have features that provided recipes as well as location for the items needed within the store.

Earlier on, there was another company that has tried to build a Videocart but failed because of poor execution. The Retailing Insights company was determined to do it right by equipping their carts with latest technologies. As such the company was funded by Angel Investor who gave them $50,000 seed money. Seed money refers to the initial investment given to a firm. The angel investor emphasized that Retailing Insights must conduct a feasibility study of the market before embarking on product development. This compelled Retailing Insights to develop a detailed description of Videocart. This included all the benefits of the product to both the retailers of grocery store and manufacturers of the product. The description was presented to both the manufacturers and retailers who were surprised by what they found out. It was unfortunate that neither party was interested in their product. The major concern for the manufacturers and retailers was the failure of the previous carts. They were both wary of trying another version of a product that had already failed. This meant that Retailing Insights had to establish its own test sites to convince the manufacturers and retailers that the product was reliable. This was to be done at their Retailing Insights' expense. Manufacturers cited the change of advertising medium as the only way that would make them be willing to come on board. According to them, a new advertising medium would have provided the scale to justify the cost of incurring related expenses as well as producing the ads. This stipulation compelled Retailing Insights to seek for the sign-up of all the grocery stores to make manufacturers excited about their product.

After careful consideration of these obstacles, Retailing Insights abandoned the idea of Videocarts. However, after brainstorming sessions, the company thought that it still had core competences and decided to take another totally different direction. A core competence is a capability or resource that acts as the source of the competitive advantage of the firm over its rivals. They conceived a new idea in area of miniature electronics where they were to build rugged transmitters that could be placed on clothing or helmets of athletes. The transmitters were to be used

*Continued*

**Feasibility of Satellite Phones: Were They Feasible?—cont'd**

alongside a set of antennas in the field to determine the location of athlete at any one time during a contest. The devices were capable of generating real-time data such as percentage of time spent by defensive lineman on the side of the opponent during a football match. These data were to be fed to broadcasters to liven the information aired during the sports broadcast. To test the feasibility of the idea, the company changed its name from Retailing Insights to Trakus. The Trakus company demonstrated a detailed simulation of the device to the potential clientele. The results of the product reception were overwhelmingly positive. The company developed the product and since then, they have been receiving venture capital financing for device development, which are normally tested in National Hockey Leagues and thoroughbred horse racing sports. The videos are available at www.trakus.com to show how the device operates.

If they had gone with their initial idea of videocarts with a feasibility study, Trakus could have spent millions of dollars only for the product to fail terribly in the marketplace. The feasibility study provided them with the information of viability of the product in the marketplace. It gave them a candid assessment of the viability of their business idea before any consumption of resources such as money and time. To its credit, Trakus responded by moving on to a totally new and viable product and this propelled the company to a more promising direction.

The founder of Silicon Graphics, Jim Clark, affirms the importance of conducting a feasibility study. Clark is blunt in his valuation of feasibility analysis, especially the importance of going out and talking to the target customers on your conceived idea. He believes that the reason why most companies fail is because the people involve to ignore the fact that some products can fail to sell in their target market. One should not be pragmatic on whether people should pay for your developed product. Once you conceive an idea about a service or a product, it is critical for you to test the market. Engage with your target customers to know exactly what they want. A product cannot do everything for everyone. Many engineers often make mistakes where they try to put everything into their conceived idea. It is imperative to go out and talk to as many clients as you can and display a copy of the product in front of them to see and note their feedback.

Jesse Livermore (1877–1940) on his reflections about market and its potential noted that "Nobody should be puzzled as to whether a market is a bull or bear market after it fairly starts. The trend is evident to a man who has an open mind and reasonable clear sight, for it is never wise for a speculator to fit his facts to his theories. Such a man will, or ought to, know whether it is a bull or a bear market, and if he knows that he knows whether to buy or to sell. It is therefore at the very inception of the movement that a man needs to know whether to buy or to sell."

## Benefits of Conducting a Feasibility Analysis for the Product/Service

1. *Helps the entrepreneur get the product right*: In this case, it will be easier to know what the customers want because you have asked them and you tested quality and usability of the product based on users' experience.
2. *Emergence of an early adopter (beta) community*: The individuals or firms that participate in feasibility analysis will in most cases become first customers. These will provide additional feedback as the service or product rolls out.
3. *Prevention of obvious flaws during the design of the service/product*: Any attempt to ask the prospective customers to test the service or products plays a major role in uncovering the obvious design flaws.
4. *Efficient use of capital and time*: Since the feasibility analysis enables the entrepreneur has a better idea of the customer needs, a lot of money and time will not be wasted in chasing ideas that will be rejected by the customers.
5. *Provides insight into addition service and/or product offerings*: A feasibility analysis for a single product or service will in most cases lead the entrepreneur to recognition of additional products and/or services.

## How to Test a Business Idea

- Think profitability
  A new venture should start by the drive toward profitability. Entrepreneur should think about the fastest way of achieving profitability even if it means slightly deviating from original goal. This is achieved by first deciding on resources available to spend and devoting about 65% of it toward driving profitability, 10% on scale, and remaining 25% on resources such as staff.
- Make failure efficient
  Failed business is when profitability is not achieved within 3 months after the start of full operation of the business. This can be referred to as "efficient failure." The time frames for businesses to pick up varies, and as such an entrepreneur should evaluate the amount of profitability attained and level of dedication and investment to the company. If the business is not profitable at all, then there is an opportunity to start another one.
- Building a minimum viable product and running it via a group of critics
  This entails making the actual product to test in the market and taking it to the target customers. Choose about 50 people who are appealed by the product and another 50 who are skeptical about the same product. Note down their feedback and work on the product based on the responses.

## Components of Feasibility Analysis

Feasibility analysis is composed of four main areas. These are the product/service feasibility, industry/market feasibility, organizational/social feasibility, and financial feasibility (Bridge & O'Neill, 2012).

## *Product/Service Feasibility Analysis*

This entails assessment of the overall appeal of a proposed service or product. Before embarking on development of the prospective service or product, a company should ensure that whatever is being developed is what their target customers want, hence they will have enough market. It is easy for an entrepreneur when launching a new venture to face challenges such as hiring employees, signing leases, raising money, buying office accessories, and writing press releases among others. This is understandable. Nevertheless, many firms will measure their success based on the capability to deliver superior service or product. According to Misra (2015), the most critical thing that an entrepreneur should consider while completing the feasibility analysis of the product/service is to go to the streets and talk to the potential customers. The success or failure of a new product or service is done before proceeding to product development.

### *Product/Service Feasibility Analysis Tests*

There are two primary tests carried out during product/service feasibility analysis: usability testing and concept testing.

#### Concept Testing

Concept testing entails the preliminary description of the idea for the service or product to the prospective clients to gauge their purchase intent, desirability, and interest. For instance, Retailing Insights abandoned their Videocart idea after the concept test. The concept testing involves three main purposes (Yalcin, 2014). First, the concept test validates the underlying premise of the service of product idea. This is majorly done by presenting the concept test to target customers in the form of a small questionnaire. The test should include questions on features, price, and prompts on how the customers think that the concept can be improved. Second, the concept test plays a major role in idea development where the entrepreneur presents the idea to prospective customers, notes the feedback, tweaks the idea, and presents it to some other customers to get additional feedback. This may be repeated severally to strengthen the idea. Third, concept test helps in estimating the market share that might be commanded by the product or service. This is summarized further.

| Validation of the Underlying Premise for the Product/Service Idea | Help in Idea Development | Help in Estimation of Sales |
|---|---|---|
| Done by giving small questionnaires to the client asking them to give their comments on how they think the idea can be improved. | Depending on results of the concept test, an entrepreneur can tweak the idea and show the revised concept to the next group of customers. This can be repeated severally to strengthen the idea. | Concept tests always seek for buying intention and this is majorly to help determine the number of people who will actually purchase the product or service. |

An example of the buying intention questions in the survey questionnaire.

If this product is developed, would you be able to buy?

1. I will definitely buy.
2. I will probably buy.
3. I might or might not buy.
4. I will probably not buy.
5. I will definitely not buy.

The entrepreneur uses the number of clients who will definitely buy or probably buy to gauge the customer interest. The number from this exercise is somehow optimistic since not everyone who says that he/she intends to purchase a product will actually buy. Nonetheless, to some extent, the numbers will give a perspective of the degree of customer interest in the product or service. If the potential customers are dispersed geographically, one can consider using some online platforms for collection of survey data. A concept test should have a **concept statement** that should have the following:

- *Description of the service or product offered*: In this section, the features of the product or service are given in a detailed manner, this may as well include the sketch and computer simulation.
- *Intended target market*: This lists the people or businesses who are expected to purchase the service or product.
- *Benefits of the service or product*: This section outlines the benefits of the service or product and details how the service or the product will add value to the customer.
- *Product/service positioning relative to rival products/services*: This describes how the service or product is positioned relative to the competitors.
- *Selling and distribution*: This section specifies the selling of the products either through distributors or directly by the manufacturer.

### Usability Testing

After the concept testing, a prototype or product model is normally developed. This physically depicts the new product that is still in tentative or rough mode. A prototype is crucial for products like board game to get a feedback that is more substantive than it can be attained from a mere concept statement. A prototype is also necessary if one has to get feedback from the potential product licensees or attendees during trade shows. In some cases, a virtual prototype can be used as it is cheaper than the physical one. However, it is in judgment call on an entrepreneur to determine whether to have a physical or virtual prototype. The main benefit of a prototype is that it helps in usability testing. The usability testing of the product/service feasibility analysis entails measurement of the user's perception of the product and ease of use (Bell, 2014). Usability tests are also referred to as beta tests, field trials, or user tests based on the circumstances involved. Usability tests can take various forms. Some people or firms working with limited budgets may develop prototypes and ask friends, family, and colleagues to use the product and give their feedback. Though fairly rudimentary, this approach appears more superior than failing to do any testing. Other may use elaborate programs and facilities in usability testing. Most of the usability testing is majorly done for products like new software and website design (Darwish, 2014).

### *Industry/Market Feasibility*

This analysis assesses the overall market appeal of the proposed product or service. This should take into consideration the attractiveness of the industry, the niche market identification, and market timeliness (Barringer, 2012).

#### *Attractiveness of the Industry*

Industries tend to vary considerably on the basis of growth rate. Industries will grow more attractively when its new products and new entrants are received well by the clients. Attractiveness of the industry is the main determinant of the feasibility of a venture. As such, many venture capitalists like Don Valentine will first assess industry attractiveness of a new start-up before funding a new venture.

**Characteristics of attractive industry are the following**:

- Large and growing where growth emphasized than the size.
- Is important to the customer where they sell products or service that a customer "must have" instead of "would like to have," and this implies that the product has an inelastic demand (this means that the quantity of good/services demanded by the buyers remain about the same level when the price changes, e.g., goods/services for daily usage).
- Fairly young instead of older or even mature. Young industry has early product life cycle with less intense competition in prices.

- High operating margins as opposed to low meaning that they are more profitable for competition and new entry.
- Are not crowded: a crowded market with many competitors will experience low operating margins and fierce competition in prices.

Though this is an ideal list, the level at which the growth possibilities of a proposed business satisfy these criteria must be clearly considered. For instance, an entrepreneur can have the idea of new service or product that fits the needs of certain clients but the market may not be big enough to support a business. The entrepreneurs may sometimes err by emphasizing so much on overall attractiveness and size of the industry they are entering, and this makes the industry attractiveness become a careful balancing act (Bridge & O'Neill, 2012).

It is advisable that entrepreneurs to avoid explaining the attractiveness of their potential markets in terms of huge markets and anticipate to get at least 1–2% of multibillion dollar markets for their business to be viable. Size alone cannot be used to evaluate the viability of the business. A start-up cannot be guaranteed to get a certain percentage of the market unless there are some real advantages over the competitors such as good access to customers and methods of imitation prevention among other things (Tito & Anderson, 2013).

For an entrepreneur to fully understand the dynamics of industry to gauge their level of attractiveness, both primary and secondary research are critical. A primary research is the original research done by the entrepreneur by talking to key industry participants and potential customers. On the other hand, a secondary research probes the already collected data. The secondary data can be acquired from government's statistics, industry-related publications, industry reports, and competitors' websites. Also, the entrepreneur should make use of authoritative sources of industry-related data available in hard copy or online. Hard copy data are very important while seeking for funding and you want to support some claims.

It is impossible to conduct a market analysis of industries that are nonexistent. Confronting entrepreneurs who are having breakthrough services or products are quite challenging. Most of the breakthrough products and services tend to establish new markets such as Yahoo, eBay, and Google. On the other hand, new service and products by feature the incremental improvement to the existing ones such as a more improved DVD player. In view of this, it is critical for a firm to conduct a primary research so as to determine whether there is sufficient market for the proposed service or product (Jayawarna, Jones, & Macpherson, 2015).

*Market Timeliness*

This entails consideration of the timeliness of introducing a certain product or service. This depends on whether the product introduced is a breakthrough or new product.

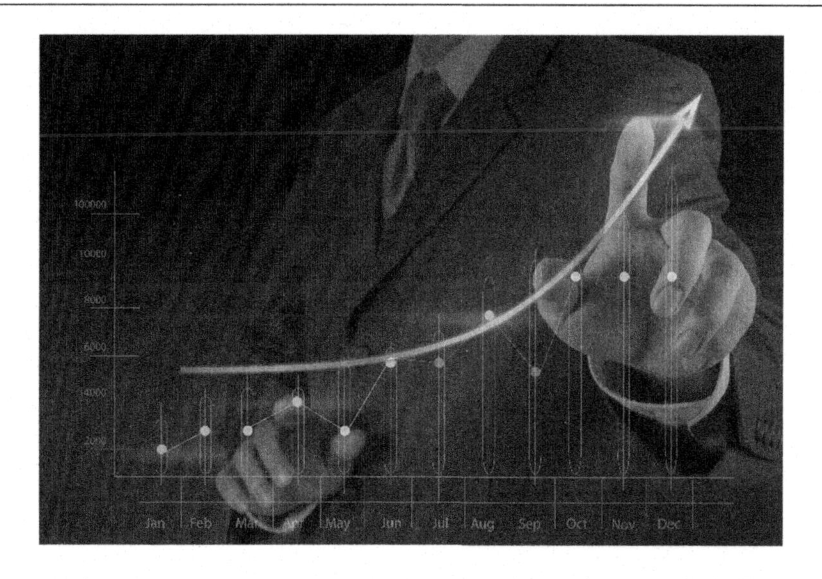


If the product is an improvement of those that already exist, determine whether there is room for the new product. Some markets are either dominated by competitors or saturated with competitors, such as the Internet search engines. Some markets like eateries are always receptive for new entrants. Another important consideration is the study of the marketplace economics to determine the dynamics of industry and gauge whether it is good to start a new business. For instance, a computer industry that is consolidating should look at the acquisition of other similar industries such as acquisition of Compaq by Hewlett–Packard in 2001, acquisition of eMachines by Gateway in 2004, and acquisition of Alienware by Dell in 2006. Any industry that consolidates have handful of big companies acquiring the major market and this forces the smaller firms out of business. Such a trend in computer industry implies that the time is not the best to launch a new firm. For new businesses developing a breakthrough product or service, the idea of whether to capture the first-mover advantage is critical. A first-mover advantage will in most cases lead to insurmountable gains as the product moves into the market (Alalawi & Alali, 2015). Nevertheless, the issue on whether getting to the market first is advantageous remains a topic under contention. Some proponents of first-mover advantage believe that most first movers set the standards for industry and will enjoy advantages of market power and brand recognition. On the other hand, the second-mover advantage describes advantages of the second entrant over the first entrant product or service. The proponents of second-mover items argue that second-mover products or services have the advantage of studying the challenges facing the first mover, hence resulting to more improved and better services or product.

### *Identification of Niche (Vertical) Market*

This is the final step in feasibility analysis of the market/industry.

A niche market represents a place within the larger market comprising of a narrower group of clients with similar needs. Most entrepreneurial firms that are successful do not begin by selling to big markets. Rather, they start by identifying the markets that are underserved or are emerging within a larger market. Another way of identifying the market is through analysis of the **horizontal** and **vertical** markets. A vertical market is analogous to niche market and it focuses on identifying similar businesses with specialized or specific needs such as development of accounting software specifically for small coffee outlets or eateries. On the other hand, a horizontal market should meet the specific needs of several different industries. For start-ups, selling into a vertical or niche market is recommended mainly because it allows the firm to establish in the industry without competition from major participants (Ashrafi, Sharma, Al-Badi, & Al-Gharbi, 2014). Also, a niche strategy gives a firm the opportunity to focus on serving a market that is specialized in a better way rather than doing everything for everybody within the broader market. The main challenge in identification of attractive vertical or niche market is that the market should be large enough to support the proposed business but should be, at the same time, small to prevent the head-to-head competition within the industry leaders. If it is impossible to clearly identify a niche market, then the envisioning of the market/industry feasibility might be a challenge for a new business venture.

### *Organizational Feasibility Analysis*

The organizational feasibility analysis entails determination of whether the proposed business is having sufficient organizational competence, management expertise, and resources so as to successfully launch the business. The two major factors to consider while conducting the organizational feasibility analysis include the resource sufficiency and management prowess (Ward, 2011).

### *Management Prowess*

A company is supposed to evaluate the ability or prowess of the management team. This requires a detailed introspection where the entrepreneur is supposed to complete a self-assessment. The two factors that are most important in ability assessment include the passion of the entrepreneur or the management team toward the business idea as well as the extent to which the management team or entrepreneur understands the market in which it is to operate. This area does not have practical substitutes for strengths (Blank, 2013).

Though financing is important, the level of importance of passion for business and customer knowledge supersedes it. If one has a great business and is aware of the customers, then there is what it takes to be a winner. However, if one has a lousy business idea, the availability of finances may not be an avenue to win. When evaluating the prowess of the management team, several other factors need to be considered. Entrepreneurs with extensive social and professional networks are able to reach to a large pool of people who are critical in helping them plug knowledge or experience gaps. Additionally, potential new venture should clearly stipulate the team that is required which comprises the new venture team. A **new venture team** refers to a group of key players, advisers, and founders who either manage or assist in management of new business during the start-up years. The new venture team should identify individuals who are capable and knowledgeable to lend credibility to organizational viability of the new venture. These people join the board of advisers or board of directors (Neck & Greene, 2011).

### *Resource Sufficiency*

This forms the second part of feasibility analysis of the organization. The resource sufficiency analysis entails evaluation of the venture to determine whether the resources are sufficient to successfully move forward and develop the new service or product. The focus in this context is on nonfinancial resources. Several areas should be assessed, including the office space available, labor pool quality, and possibility of accessing the intellectual property protection on major aspects of the business. Some new ventures are able to minimize the initial expenses of the facility and gain access to resources by locating themselves within a business incubator. One of the main resource adequacies that a firm should consider is the proximity to other similar firms for the sake of business clusters. Clusters play a major role in increasing the productivity of the firms since the employees can easily network with one another. Also, the firms in a cluster can easily access scientific knowledge, technological expertise, and specialized suppliers. To test for resource sufficiency, a firm should list at least six nonfinancial resources that are most critical and which will be required for them to move the business idea forward. If the critical resources are unavailable, proceeding with the business idea may be impractical (Ward, 2011).

### *Financial Feasibility Analysis*

This forms the final stage of a detailed feasibility analysis. The analysis entails quick assessment of the financials. Since the business specifics will inevitably evolve, more rigor at this point may not be necessary. It is impractical to spend too much time to prepare detailed financial forecasts. An entrepreneur should concentrate on getting the total start-up capital, financial attractiveness of the venture, and how similar businesses perform financially (Lee & Andrade, 2011).

If the proposed venture moves past the feasibility analysis stage, there will be need to complete the projected financial statements that demonstrated the projected financial viability of the firm in the first 3 years.

#### *Total Start-Up Capital Required*

This refers to total amount of money required for the business to make its first sale. The entrepreneur should prepare an actual budget that lists all the expected operating expenses and capital purchases to generate the first revenues. At the beginning, only few businesses quality for either equity funds or bank financing. Rather, the financial feasibility analysis should clearly outline where the new venture will get the funds from. If friends and families will fund the venture, or if credit cards and home equity line of credit will be used, there should be a reasonable plan to pay back the money. In case the bank or equity investors are involved, the plan should be done in such a way that the start-up money will be enough up to the point when the cash flow will be positive.

Outlining how the start-up costs for a new firm will be covered is very critical. Many ventures may look promising but they lack ways of raising the enough funds to get the business to fully operational level or even recover all the costs involved during start-up (Barringer, 2012). Murphy's law is common in start-up venture—things will have to go wrong. It is almost impossible to get a start-up that does not have setbacks before it is fully operational. In most cases, the start-ups suffer from unanticipated delays and expenses before getting to the market.

*Financial Performance of Other Similar Businesses*

This forms the second component of the financial feasibility analysis. This process entails estimation of potential financial performance of the proposed start-up by comparing it to other similar established businesses. This gives approximate numbers rather than exact. The exercise can be carried out using little ethical detective tasks. First, make use of various reports that are available, some for free while some are paid for. The reports offer detailed analysis of the trends as well as reports for various individual firms. Some websites allow the use to give the projected revenue after which they get a mock income statement that shows expense and profitability percentages for the business in the same category. Also, entrepreneurs can easily track sales data by reviewing and observing the public records. A basic way of achieving this is by frequent visit to the similar business and having a general overview of the number of clients coming in and out within a day. This analysis provides the entrepreneur with a general perspective of the financial performance of firms similar to the proposed venture (Bridge & O'Neill, 2012). This is admittedly challenging for a start-up. The information gotten during this stage of analysis can also be utilized in preparation of pro forma statements at later dates.

*Overall Financial Attractiveness of the Prospective Venture*

The overall financial attractiveness of a venture is evaluated based on the projected rate of return of the venture. At the feasibility stage, projected rate of return entails the comparison of the proposed venture to other similar businesses. Pro forma statements can be prepared to include financial projections for 1–3 years to give a more precise estimation. This should be accompanied by the respective financial ratios. This may be done during the business planning development stage to save on time in feasibility stage. Several factors have to be considered when investigating whether the return projected is enough to justify launching of the business. These include the following:

- the amount of money invested;
- time required in earning the return;
- risks assumed when launching the venture;
- existing alternative for invested money;
- existing alternatives for the efforts and time of the entrepreneur.

Conclusions should be made after evaluating of the aforementioned factors. For instance, opportunities that demand substantial capital and require long maturity periods may have a lot of risks involved unless their rate of return is very high. For instance, it would be unrealistic for entrepreneurs to invest $10 million in a start-up that is capital intensive and risky and only earns 5% rate of return. The 5% can easily be earned through the money market fund with minimal or no risk. Adequacy of returns is also dependent on the alternatives of the people involved. For instance, an individual contemplating of leaving a $140,000-per-year job to start a venture that will need a higher rate of return than the person leaving a $40,000-per-year job.

A list of the most important parts of the feasibility study is presented in Table 3.1.

*Business Performance Management in the Context of "New Business Era"*

In the modern business environment, the dynamic nature of business has compelled business managers to come up with various strategies to remain relevant in the industry. This is

**Table 3.1: The Main Components of a Good Feasibility Study**

| No. | Section | Short Description |
| --- | --- | --- |
| 1 | Executive summary | This part will be written at the end of the study and should cover: background of the problem, purpose of the study, brief details of the approach/method, important results and/or findings, and the major conclusion. |
| 2 | The purpose of the feasibility study | "A well-defined problem is half solved" states an old saying. Likewise, in this section must be defined the business problem and/or the business opportunity as well as those who will contribute. |
| 3 | The analysis (market, technical, financial, and social feasibility) | In this section of the study explained the present method of implementation (for example, a product or service, system, procedure, etc.), the strengths, and weaknesses of your approach as well as the aspects in regard to four feasibility factors. |
| 4 | Requirements | Having in mind the project's focus and characteristics, one will define here the requirements (for example, to produce a chair the requirements are different than for building a house). |
| 5 | The approach | In this part of the study, one will present the solution or solutions and/or course of action and will motivate the choice. It is possible that different scenarios with viable options will be presented here. |
| 6 | Evaluation | In this section must be analyzed the cost-effectiveness of the approach (step 4). One might start with estimated total cost of the project. |

Note: At the end, it is recommended that you revisit all the components of the feasibility plan and made necessary adjustments, if necessary. It might be useful to request the opinion of a mentor or trusted advisor on your work.

necessitated by the business needs to make profits, beat their competitors, and importantly, satisfy the shareholders and customers. To achieve this, business leaders have recognized the role played by innovation in performance.

According to business analysts, while managing business, organizations have to align innovation with the business objectives that they have set for themselves. As such, the management has to ensure that it gives equal attention to innovation and business, and at the same time, foster the culture of creativity in business. Given that there is no universally agreed upon way of managing this, Belenzon (2010) asserts that there are a number of ways that can be applied to yield equally attractive results. In the modern business environment, many organizations have taken the option of jointly developing products and technology, which creates a path for expansion and improved productivity. This does not forgo the necessity to foster in-built innovation from the employees, as well as the top management. Additionally, while aligning business performance and innovation, there has to be a delicate balance between the internal organizational environment and the external industrial environment. This is to avoid having conflicting resolutions to making a profitable and sustainable business model.

However, despite the wide documentation of the association between innovation and business performance, business management specialists assert that modern organizations are yet to fill the gap of success. This means that business performance and innovation are not only textbook decisions, rather scientific and artistic undertakings. Most of the large businesses that have successfully integrated innovation into their business culture have records of exhaustive and detailed research into the elements of success in their respective industries. According to the available evidence, the most successful companies are those that make a holistic and systematic approach to business innovation.

Modern businesses are under constant pressure to change their approach in the dynamic business environment. According to Dunning (2014), given the nature of globalization and the ever-increasing customer demand, businesses have to ensure that they structure their operations to satisfy all stakeholders involved. At the same time, the competitive force in business industry mounts the pressure on organizations to improve their operations. This, among many other challenges makes it imperative for the businesses to improve their performance management, so to remain relevant in the industry. The techniques that were used earlier on have been outdated, and the businesses have no option but to improve their innovative approach toward effective business performance management.

The main aim of present section is to enlarge the knowledge database in regard to business performance management and innovation. While at it, the findings will be significant for business analysts and practitioners for determining the direction that the shift in the business sector is taking. This is based on the analysis of strategies that various business managers have used to improve the productivity of their respective firms. At the same time, the findings will give a hint on the challenges that modern businesses are facing, pertaining to embracing innovation in increasing productivity, competitiveness, and industrial relevance. At the same time, the purpose of this section is also to investigate the successes and failures of the strategies that have been used by modern business models, which is the first step toward increased efficiency in the endeavor.

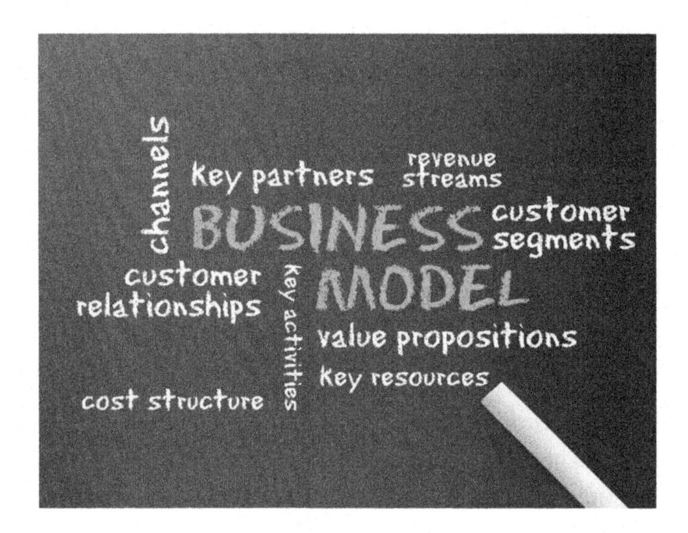


Nowadays, with all the changes and variations in the business world and the increased need for innovation and creativity, the business model topic has an increased popularity among business professionals. In simple words, a business model can be defined as a strategic plan about how the business entity makes or plans to make money. Making money for the company is the main responsibility of the manager. The business model term is strictly related to innovative ways or innovation in regard to earning money on behalf of the business entity. One of the most creative, efficient, and innovative business model is the canvas business model (created by Alexander Osterwalder). For a business model to be successful in Middle East, it needs a more personal approach and to consider all the elements in regard to local specificities.

Having as source of inspiration Osterwalder's canvas business model, the author has developed a business model suitable for the GCC area, taking into consideration area's specificities and the knowledge acquired during consulting services for different companies in Middle East. The model with explanations is presented in the Annex 1.

It is relevant to mention here the difference between a business model and a business plan. A **business plan** is a road map, which shows all the steps for company or a business idea to achieve its purpose/success; it can serve also as managerial tool. A **business model**, as it was mentioned before, it is all about how the company makes or plans to make money.

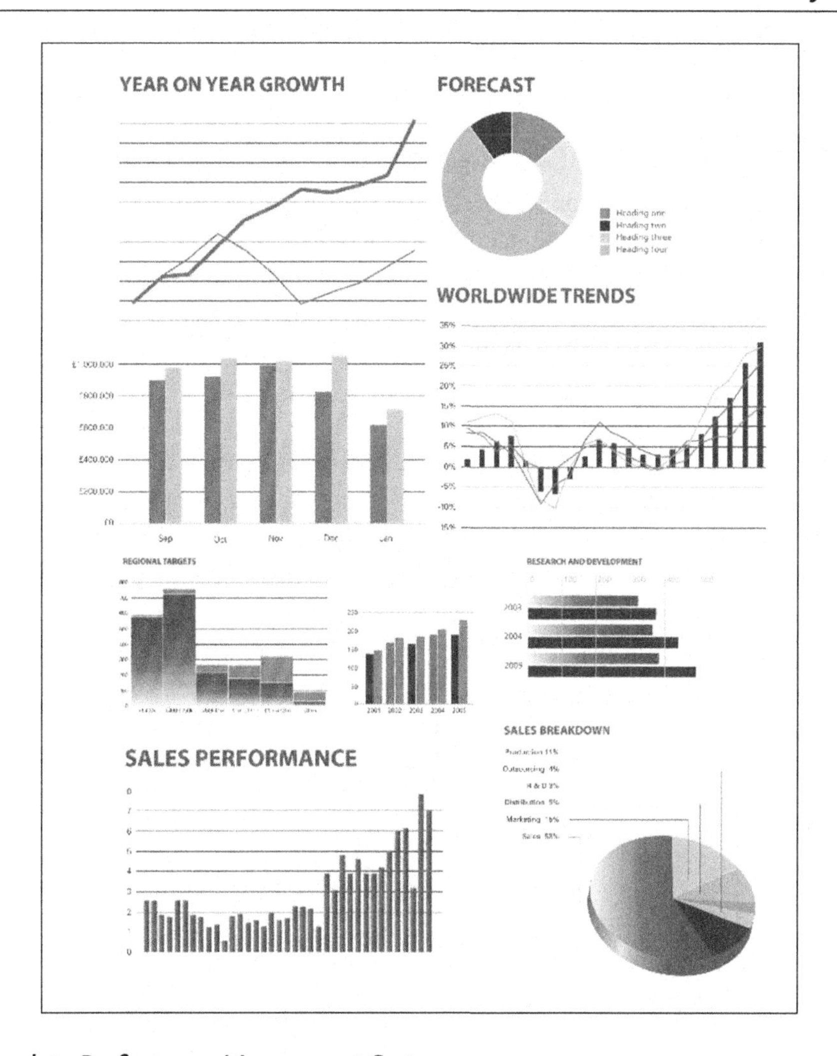


*New Approach to Performance Management System*

Zott (2010) identifies the importance of having the right resources for the purposes of surviving in the modern turbulent business environment. While these resources can be obtained through the input of the management, some of them take the effort of research and investment to obtain. One of these resources is financial ability. Demil (2010) asserts that financial resources are the backbone to obtaining almost every other resource that a business needs to grow. The financial resources come in the form of the organization's liquidity, investments from the shareholders, donor funds, and others, such as loans. In the modern business environment, a strong financial capability is indicative of a stronger competitive position, regardless the nature of industry which a business is operating in.

According to Stroh (2011), human resource is still the most important asset in business. The management is compelled to recognize that the people working for the organization hold the major key to success, as they determine the general direction that the productivity trend takes. While most organizations may lack the right human resource at the beginning, there are a number of innovative ways of obtaining just the right people for the right job. These include continuous training, expatriate assignments, and outsourcing (Downes, 2010). Similarly, to improve the capability of the human resources, the management has to pay attention to internal and external forces that shape the organizational environment, which is key to obtaining and retaining the best human resource. According to Claessens (2012), a business that has a strong financial capability, backed by an able human resource, is able to withstand the pressures facilitated by increased competition and globalization.

*Strategic and Tactical Planning*

Teece (2010) highlights the role of strategy in innovation. According to Teece (2010), strategy should be viewed as the process that the management uses to accomplish certain organizational objectives. Before recommending a certain strategy to the organizational leadership, it is the role of the management to evaluate the possible methods that can be used, at the same time, measuring them against industrial forces. While doing this, Nickels (2011) asserts that the management has to factor in elements such as competitive differentiation, conduct an SWOT analysis, and evaluate the business' position in the market, before going ahead with a certain strategy. As such, while undertaking a strategic planning process, the management has to highlight the business' strengths, and back this up with innovative approaches, to come up with the best strategy to achieve organizational objectives.

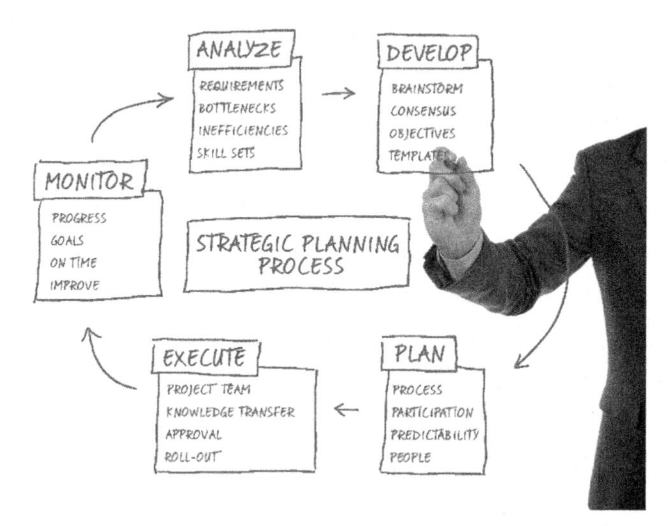


In business management, Casadesus-Masanell and Ricart (2010) defines tactical planning as the initiatives, techniques, and decisions that are needed to help the management utilize the resources in a way that they will achieve organizational objectives. While making tactical plans, the organization's managers develop new approaches to help the organization tackle existing challenges and make room for more improvement. According to Frezatti (2011), tactical planning also involves evaluation of the existing methodologies at every level of the organization and assesses their capacity to contribute to the general organizational development. Longenecker (2013) labels technical plans as short-term actions that organizations take mainly because they are used to break down the whole picture into smaller easily comprehensible fragments. As such, a good tactical plan is one with measurable and achievable short-term goals, however, with bolder objective in the long run.

### *Impact of Innovation on Business Performance Management*

Melville (2010) says that one of the most important roles of innovation is creating a new environment and opportunities for business growth. This is because innovation introduces new aspects and different approaches to tackling daily business organization matters. As such, authors and business analysts maintain that innovation is the single most vital element of business expansion. According to Kanter (2001), innovation is a part of technology management in organizations. Regardless, managers have to ensure that their innovative capacities taken into consideration the organizational objectives, and any challenges that may limit their usefulness. At the same time, the role of innovation in moving products and services into the market shall not be overlooked, as it forms the basis for measuring the success or failure of an organization.

Zott (2010) describes innovation as a strategic human resource imperative. This is because innovation demonstrates the will of the management to propagate their ideas and vision for the organization. As such, the human resource leaders have to recognize the fact that hiring, organizational culture, and training, all which are part of productivity enhancement, are guided by innovation. While picking the right people for the right job, the human resource managers have to ensure that they can identify those with the ability to "think outside the box" and come up with solutions to standing challenges (Dahlen, 2010). This can only be achieved by embracing and practicing innovation at the organization.

Valdiserri (2010) argues that a successful company is one that realizes the role of innovation and implements it to achieve profitability and stronger competitive advantage. While management innovation includes administrative and organizational tasks, innovation helps the business to implement developments that are geared toward success. On the same note, López-Nicolás and Meroño-Cerdán (2011) asserts that innovative process has a direct positive influence on organization's performance management, as it entails creation of an environment that embraces change and business transformation.

Businesses are increasingly using technology to boost their innovation. While taking into consideration internal factors such as organizational values and human resource, modern businesses are considering external factors, such as industrial competition and growing customer demand. Using this to set their standards, managers have embraced the role that is played by technology in improving productivity and efficiency. At the same time, the modern business organizations have factored the role played by the changing product costs and utility, and as such, came up with innovative ways of managing critical organizational resources. As identified in the literature review part corroborated with conclusions/results from author's field experience, the main organizational resources that support innovation are human resource and financial resources. By helping businesses to align business strategies with cost-effective technology, innovation has proven the key to success in the modern business environment.

Different companies have the liberty of choosing their techniques to boost productivity. However, studies have shown that years of marketing research and commitment to organizational objectives hold the key to fruitful innovation. While some companies concentrate on selling their brand image, others use innovation to boost the productivity of their workforce, and generally, the success of their firms. At the same time, other organizations use innovation to manage their finances, which is a strategy to reduce costs attributed to poor budgeting. The present business environment and conditions prove that the execution of strategy factors elements such as capital, organizational systems, human resources, and other metrics that are required for success. The bottom line remains that business leaders have to align their organizational capability with whichever strategies they choose to come up with innovative ways of managing their performance.

A more recent research on activity-based costing (ABC) method contribution to business performance indicates the benefits and limitations of adopting the method within business companies. There are two major benefits from the adoption of this method: allowance of ABC to fully scrutinize the whole production progressions and enables corporations to alter the combination of products manufactured and clients attended, enabling them to concentrate on the gainful products and productive consumers. Despite the benefits, the administrators should know the system has some restrictions. At times it is hard to openly differentiate the various activities, resource utilization or product cost. Exclusion of any cost related to the product or service is another challenge that might appear. Activities costs such as distribution, promotion, research and enlargement, and product trade are also usually excluded in products' cost. Although these kinds of cost are direct and can be attributable to certain product or service, ABC application is expensive and at times it may pose a challenge in appearance of several activities (Pauceanu & Hisam, 2016).

As a result of literature review in regard to business performance and author's experience as business consultant and over the years built expertise in entrepreneurship, small business management and organizational management, the following recommendations are to be made for the companies who consider their improved performance as first priority:

1. Business leaders should accelerate their firms' transformation through IT innovation. In the modern business environment, top companies need IT leadership that has the drive to change the functioning of the entire organization. A fast-growing successful company

is the one that is *characterized* by paramount utilization of IT resources and assets, keeping in mind the global trends in the same.

2. There should be constant evaluation of business resources (human and material) to tell the business' position in the current business environment.
   At one point or another, organizations need to revisit their records to evaluate the condition of their resources. This means that the management needs to revise records of their human and material resources from time to time and make necessary changes whenever necessary. Management analysts identify this as one of the major functions of the human resource department. Another important element is employees' satisfaction, which is a vital element for business performance and survival.
3. Customers, shareholders, and all other stakeholders in the business should be involved in the innovative process.
   Collective action is born out of a unified effort by all stakeholders. Customers play the key role of guiding the business to make improvements to their products and services. On the other hand, the shareholders hold the key to financial investment, which is needed for innovation to be actualized.
4. Organizational plans should always be aligned with business objectives, so as to avoid unsustainable development through innovation.
   While making innovative decisions about businesses, the management is supposed to ensure that every decision made is sustainable. This is to avoid having conflict of interest in the future, as it may hinder the organization from making any further progress. Sustainable innovation creates an opportunity for further growth.

## Chapter Three Summary

1. Feasibility analysis refers to the process of assessing a business idea to determine whether it is viable. It is the preliminary evaluation of an idea done to determine whether it is worth pursuing an idea.
2. The most appropriate time to conduct a feasibility analysis is during the early stages of idea inception and follows the opportunity recognition that normally comes before developing a business plan.
3. The product/service feasibility analysis entails the assessment of the overall service or product appeal. The two primary tests considered in this type of feasibility analysis include concept and usability testing.
4. A concept statement refers to the preliminary description of the venture idea.
5. The three main purposes of concept test include validation of underlying premises that are behind a service or product idea, facilitate idea development, and enhance the assessment of potential market share that a service or product commands.
6. The usability testing entails asking the users of a service or product to perform some tasks so as to measure the ease of use of the product as well as the satisfaction and perception of the users based on experience.

7. The feasibility analysis of the market/industry entails assessing the overall market appeal for the service or product that is being proposed. There are three main factors that should be considered during the market/industry feasibility analysis. These include the industry attractiveness, niche market identification, and market timeliness.
8. Primary research entails the original research conducted by an entrepreneur. When assessing the attractiveness of the market, the primary research involves the entrepreneur talking to the key industry participants or potential clients. Secondary research helps in discovering meaning in or from the data that have already been collected.
9. The organizational feasibility analysis is done to determine the sufficiency of the management expertise, resources, and organizational competence of the proposed business. The main factors considered in organizational feasibility analysis include the resource sufficiency and management prowess.
10. The financial feasibility analysis refers to the preliminary analysis of the finances of a business to determine the financial soundness of the proposed business. The main factors considered in this analysis include the financial rate of return, capital requirements, and overall attractiveness of the venture.
11. Modern businesses are under constant pressure to change their approach in the dynamic business environment. The competitive force in business industry mounts the pressure on organizations to improve their operations. This, among many other challenges, makes it imperative for the businesses to improve their performance management, so to remain relevant in the industry. The techniques that were used earlier on have been outdated, and the businesses have no option but to improve their innovative approach toward effective business performance management.

## Chapter Three Questions

### Choose Either True or False

1. An entrepreneur should conduct a feasibility study to determine how viable a business idea is before proceeding with business development.
   - *True*
   - *False*
2. A feasible venture refers to the business activity that will generate enough profits and cash flow for the business as well as withstanding the risks encountered and remains viable so as to meet the objectives of the founders.
   - *True*
   - *False*
3. Efficient business failure is when profitability is achieved within 3 months after the start of full operation of the business.
   - *True*
   - *False*

4. Product/service feasibility analysis entails the preliminary description of the idea for the service or product to the prospective clients to gauge their purchase intent, desirability, and interest.
   - *True*
   - *False*
5. Market/industry feasibility analysis assesses the overall market appeal of the proposed product or service.
   - *True*
   - *False*
6. Young industries have early product life cycle with less intense competition in prices.
   - *True*
   - *False*
7. Crowded market with many competitors is less likely to experience low operating margins and fierce competition in prices.
   - *True*
   - *False*
8. Two major factors to consider while conducting the organizational feasibility analysis include the resource sufficiency and management prowess.
   - *True*
   - *False*
9. Usability testing entails asking the users of a service or product to perform some tasks so as to measure the ease of use of the product as well as the satisfaction and perception of the users based on experience.
   - *True*
   - *False*
10. Primary research helps in discovering meaning in or from the data that have already been collected.
    - *True*
    - *False*

### *Multiple Choice Questions*

11. The main purpose of feasibility study is to determine how viable the business idea is. Which one of the following listed items is not a component of feasibility study?
    A. Operational feasibility
    B. Product/Service feasibility
    C. Financial feasibility
    D. Organizational feasibility

12. Which one of the following is a benefit of feasibility study?
    A. Provides insight into addition service and/or product offerings
    B. Efficient use of capital and time
    C. Helps the entrepreneur get the product right
    D. All the above
13. A business idea can be tested using three main methods. Which one of the following is not used in testing a business idea?
    A. Building a minimum viable product and running it via a group of critics
    B. Selling the idea to other well-equipped developers and monitor it.
    C. Make failure efficient
    D. Think profitability
14. Which are the major tests of product/service feasibility study
    A. Usability testing
    B. Concept testing
    C. Prototype testing
    D. A and B
15. Concept testing entails the preliminary description of the idea for the service or product to the prospective clients to gauge their purchase intent, desirability, and interest. There are three main purposes of concept testing as listed further. Which one is not?
    A. Idea development
    B. Sales estimation
    C. Estimation of target customer base
    D. Validation the underlying premise for the product/service idea
16. The feasibility analysis of market/industry encompasses three main components. Which one of the following listed items is not one of these components?
    A. Attractiveness of the industry
    B. Validation of the underlying premise for the product/service idea
    C. Niche market identification
    D. Market timeliness
17. The financial feasibility should include three main components. Which one of the following is not a component of financial feasibility?
    A. Overall financial attractiveness of the prospective venture
    B. Financial performance of other similar businesses
    C. Total start-up capital required
    D. None
18. How can you evaluate the overall attractiveness of a new business venture?
    A. Evaluating the projected rate of return of the venture
    B. Estimating the total profits and liabilities
    C. Estimation of initial capital
    D. Calculating the return on equity

19. Several factors have to be considered when investigating whether the return projected is enough to justify launching of the business. Which one among the following should be considered?
    A. Existing alternatives for the efforts and time of the entrepreneur
    B. Risks assumed when launching the venture
    C. The amount of money invested
    D. All the above
20. When is the most appropriate time to conduct a feasibility analysis?
    A. After idea inception but before developing a business plan
    B. Immediately after developing a business plan
    C. Before idea inception
    D. None of the above

**Note: Answers in Appendix Section.**

## References


Alalawi, A. I., & Alali, F. M. (2015). Factors affecting E-commerce adoption in SMEs in GCC: an empirical study of Kuwait. *Research Journal of Information Technology*, *7*(1), 1–21.

Ashrafi, R., Sharma, S. K., Al-Badi, A. H., & Al-Gharbi, K. (2014). Achieving business success through information and communication technologies adoption by small and medium enterprises in Oman. *Middle-East Journal of Scientific Research*, *22*(1), 138–146.

Barreto, H. (2013). *The entrepreneur in microeconomic theory: Disappearance and explanation*. Routledge.

Barringer, B. (2012). *Entrepreneurship: Successfully launching new ventures*.

Belenzon, S. (2010). Innovation in business groups. *Management Science*, *56*(3), 519–535.

Bell, J. R. (2014). *Think like an entrepreneur*. US: Palgrave Macmillan.

Blank, S. (2013). Why the lean start-up changes everything. *Harvard Business Review*, *91*(5), 63–72.

Bridge, S., & O'Neill, K. (2012). *Understanding enterprise: Entrepreneurship and small business*. Palgrave Macmillan.

Casadesus-Masanell, R., & Ricart, J. E. (2010). From strategy to business models and onto tactics. *Long Range Planning*, *43*(2), 195–215.

Claessens, S. K. (2012). How do business and financial cycles interact? *Journal of International Economics*, *87*(1), 178–190.

Dahlen, M. (2010). *Creativity unlimited: Thinking inside the box for business innovation*. John Wiley & Sons.

Darwish, S. (2014). The role of universities in developing small and medium enterprises (SMEs): future challenges for Oman. *International Business and Management*, *8*(2), 70–77.

Demil, B. L. (2010). Business model evolution: in search of dynamic consistency. *Long Range Planning*, *43*(2), 227–246.

Downes, M. V. (2010). Individual profiles as predictors of expatriate effectiveness. *Competitiveness Review: An International Business Journal*, *20*(3), 235–247.

Dunning, J. (2014). *The globalization of business (Routledge revivals): The challenges of 1990s*. Routledge.

Frezatti, F. A. (2011). Does management accounting play role in planning process? *Journal of Business Research*, *64*(3), 242–249.

Ghisi, E., & Schondermark, P. N. (2013). Investment feasibility analysis of Business. *Business Management*, *27*(7), 2555–2576.

Glackin, C. (2013). Entrepreneurship. *Starting and Operating a Small Business*, *3*, 23–28.

Goel, S., & Karri, R. (2006). Entrepreneurs, effectual logic and over-trust. *Entrepreneurship Theory and Practice*, *30*(4), 477–493.

Jayawarna, D., Jones, O., & Macpherson, A. (2015). Becoming an entrepreneur *Entrepreneurial learning. New perspectives in research, education and practice*, *4*, 20–24.

Kanter, R. (2001). From spare change to real change: the social sector as beta site for business innovation. *Harvard Business Review on Innovation*.

Lee, C. J., & Andrade, E. B. (2011). Fear, social projection, and financial decision making. *Journal of Marketing Research*, *48*, 121–129.

Longenecker, J. P. (2013). *Small business management*. Cengage Learning.

López-Nicolás, C., & Meroño-Cerdán, Á. L. (2011). Strategic knowledge management, innovation and performance. *International Journal of Information Management*, *31*(6), 502–509.

Melville, N. P. (2010). Information systems innovation for environmental sustainability. *MIS Quarterly*, *34*(1), 1–21.

Misra, P. K. (2015). Entreprenuership in new venture: a dynamic capability perspective. In The 8th International Conference for Entrepreneurship. *Innovation and Regional Development*, *27*(229), 90–94.

Neck, H. M., & Greene, P. G. (2011). Entrepreneurship education: known worlds and new frontiers. *Journal of Small Business Management*, *49*(1), 55–70.

Nickels, W. G. (2011). *Understanding business* (9th ed.). New York: McGraw-Hill.

Pauceanu, A. M., & Hisam, W. M. (2016). ABC method contribution to business performance. *International Journal of Applied Business and Economic Research*, *14*(1), 511–520.

Stroh, L. K. (2011). Making or buying employees: the relationship between human resources policy, business strategy and corporate restructuring. *Journal of Applied Business Research*, *10*(4), 12–18.

Teece, D. (2010). Business models, business strategy and innovation. *Long Range Planning*, *43*(2), 172–194.

Tito, D. A., & Anderson, G. (2013). Feasibility analysis for a manned Mars free-return mission in 2018. In *Aerospace conference*, pp. 1–18.

Valdiserri, G. W. (2010). The study of leadership in small business organizations: impact on profitability and organizational success. *The Entrepreneurial Executive*, *15*, 47.

Ward, J. L. (2011). *Keeping the family business healthy: How to plan for continuing growth, profitability, and family leadership*. Palgrave Macmillan.

Yalcin, S. (2014). SMEs: their role in developing growth and the potential for investors. *CFA Institute Conference Proceedings Quarterly*, *31*(3), 7–11.

Zott, C. A. (2010). Business model design: an activity system perspective. *Long Range Planning*, *43*(2), 216–226.

CHAPTER 4

# Business Plan

## Chapter Outline

## Introduction

A business plan, by its definition, is a detailed plan that clarifies why the business is existing; the aims for the existence, client groups, products and services, financial projections, and how it intends to develop and deliver those services and/or products. It acts as a road map for the organization and shows clearly the destination it seeks and the path to follow to get there. This should also be accompanied by a description of the resources required to complete the entrepreneurial journey.

## Types of Business Plans

There are different types of business plans. This depends on whether the business is new or existing. Choose the business plan that best suits your need based on the stage that the business is and what you want to achieve. Following are the different types on business plans:

1. **Start-up plan**: This covers all the topics that are relevant when undertaking a new venture like company formation, products, forecasts, management team, financial analysis, and strategy.
2. **Internal plan**: It is used internally in existing business and not accessible to outside parties. This plan does not necessarily require detailed analysis of the company and breakdown of the management structure. It majorly covers where the company anticipates going and how to reach there.
3. **Operations plan**: It is used in a similar way as internal plan but comprises majorly of the benchmarks such as deadlines, responsibilities of the teams, dates, and milestones.
4. **Strategic plan**: It is internal in nature and focuses mostly on setting priorities and high-level opportunities for the company.
5. **Growth/expansion plan**: This plan focuses on a specific area of the business of subset. For instance, loan application or new investments may require a detailed growth plan.

While the growth plan may be used internally, there should be comprehensive forecasts of expenses and sales for the new product or venture.

6. **Feasibility plan**: This is majorly done when considering a new start-up to evaluate the effectiveness of the idea and whether it is worth pursuing. The plan should have a summary, elements of success, mission statement, overview and analysis of the market, cost, pricing, and any probable expenses.

Business plan is indispensable while running a business. The plan should be well thought out to draw a clear picture of the targeted achievement. A good business plan will bridge the gap from the current position of the business to the future or anticipated position. Planning can be considered as one of the main step toward advancing any business activity. Planning can either be operation or strategic, or long-term or short-term. The plan is normally dependent on size and type of the business as well as the underlying mission to start up the operation (Finch, 2013).

Once a person identifies the purpose of the plan, it is easier to get started. It is critical to note that for start-ups and new ventures, a more comprehensive and traditional plan should be used. An internal plan may be used when trying to evaluate the effectiveness and efficiency of internal systems and operations. No matter the type of the plan that you chose, the fact remains that a business plan is very important tool for your entrepreneurial process.

Learning how to write a business plan is very crucial. Some of the reasons that an entrepreneur should be developing a business plan include the following:

- It is an effective tool that helps one define and focus the business objectives in a detailed and comprehensive manner.
- A business plan can be used as a selling tool when dealing with prominent relationships such as investors, banks, and lenders.

- It can be used as a tool to solicit advice and opinions from people, inclusive of those in the same field of the business even if they freely give invaluable advice.
- The plan can uncover crucial omissions and weaknesses during the planning process.

## Important Components to Tailor Into the Business Plan

- *Mission statement*: This concisely outlines your business goals and purpose.
- *You*: A person is the greatest ingredient for the business success. The entrepreneur should focus on the prior experiences that are applicable to the new business. They should be a record of resumes for each contact that comes into the business.

- *Business profile*: It is vital to define and describe the business intended and outline the services offered. Stay focused on the specialized market that you aspire to venture into.
- *Economic assessment*: It outline clearly the economic environment where the intended business is supposed to be established. This is especially critical for the regulating agencies as well as the demographics in which the person will be dealing with. You can get data on traffic flow and demographic studies from the local planning departments.
- *Assessment of cash flow*: It is crucial to include a cash flow for 1 year to depict the capital requirements. Also, include any weakness and any measures that you intend to take in case they occur.

Any person with the passion to be an entrepreneur and confidence that the move is innovative and rewarding and the capital is not enough, the business plan must be prepared in such a way that the financiers will be interested to fund the projects. It is imperative to study and get help using different avenues and individuals. It is critical to note that money is one of the components of business requirement but not the only point for one to succeed.

In the current world, it is easier for someone to access money from different sources with a sincere minimum effort. Proper documentation and professionalism of the business plan is very critical.

Nowadays, being just creative is not enough to succeed. Someone should be able to efficiently communicate the ideas and processes and, of course, being able to sell the output of creation.

It is always advisable for someone to first check his/her entrepreneural capabilities for 1–5 years and be prepared to critically think within a certain period. If one fails to reach an expected position, then one should make efforts so that the next position becomes brighter.

### *Think for Yourself*

After acquiring the certificate in your education, you are well prepared as a businessperson; you need 1–5 years of practical experience; and you should never lose your patience, faith, and determination. You may get a job, which is unsustainable and hence compelled to start a job as an entrepreneur. There is a high chance for you to start offering jobs to people with the same unsustainable salary or better. You will have an opportunity to integrate with people, change lives, and become an icon in the society. You should be the change that you would like to see in your community. The change should start with yourself.

In regard to business opportunities in GCC area, the following areas present good returns: renewable energies, tourism industry, recycling, medical industry, food industry, manufacturing industry, trade, and commerce.

*All GCC countries are as richly endowed with renewable resources as they are with hydrocarbons. Gulf countries will require 100 GW of additional power over the next 10 years to meet the increasing demand. Renewable energy offers Gulf countries a proven, homegrown path to reduce* $CO_2$ *emissions, as well.*

**Pauceanu, A.M. (2015)**

## Business Plan Format

### Executive Summary

**a.** This provides a snapshot of the business, the entrepreneur, and the rationale for taking that business initiative.
**b.** The summary should give the reader a basic understanding of the business at hand.
**c.** Provide information such as customers, product, and future plans.
**d.** Outline the specialty of the business.
**e.** Create the urge for the reader to read more.
**f.** Mention the incorporation/establishment date for the business.
**g.** Outline the nature of the product and/or services.
**h.** Describe the workforce requirement.
**i.** Give a simple summary of the financial breakdown, source of funding, and its utilization.
**j.** Limit the wordings to a single page.

### *Brief Business Description*

a. Business name
b. Nature of business
c. Industry/sector
d. Business objectives
e. Employment introduction of entrepreneur(s) giving out their names, qualifications, experience, and ownership percentage
f. Investment
g. Ownership type such as incorporated or sole proprietorship business
h. Loan and equity
i. Potential market

### *Products and Services Description*

The entrepreneur describes the products or services with the most important features being mentioned. Also, the comparative advantages and disadvantages are mentioned in this section (you can use an SWOT analysis for this purpose).

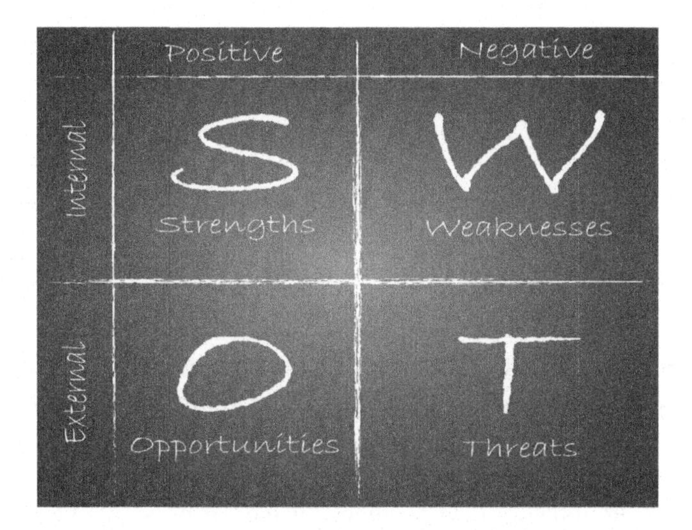


Highly detailed and technical descriptions of the product may not be necessary. You should use simple terms and do not use industry buzzwords to enable your readers to understand the content. Describe how your products will differ from those of competitors. Depending on nature of your business, the section on products and services can be very short or long. For instance, if the business is focused on more products, you may require sometime to describe the product. Also, if your key strength lies in pricing of the product, you may not need to describe your product detaily. Always determine what your key strength is and where you will be competitive.

Some of the key questions to answer in this section include the following:

a. Do your products and/or services already exist in the market?
b. What timelines are there for you to bring the products and/or services to the market?
c. What makes your products and/or services outstanding? What are the competitive advantages? What are the competitive advantages to be overcome?
d. What will you get the products and/or services? Will you manufacture? Will you assemble? Will you get from other suppliers/wholesalers? Is the supply steady after the business takes off?
e. What need are you fulfilling for your customers and how?

## Marketing Plan

A good marketing plan provides a clear concept of the market, of the potential customers, and of the ways you can reach to them. This implies the need to conduct market research and the marketing plan should be informative, specific, and with reference.

a. Conduct an analysis of the major competitors and rank them accordingly;
b. Carry out a SWOT analysis and comparison of your product or service with the competitors;
c. Mention your targeted marketing area and if there is any more to international markets, this should be mentioned.

### *How to Estimate the Target Market*

To calculate the market share, it is important to first define the size of the market that you intend to compete in. Your market may include nation or the whole world but the one that matters for a new start-up in the sphere of the influence of your business. An entrepreneur can assess the size of the target market by following the given criteria.

- **Geographic targeting**: It determines where the customers are. For instance, for a supplier, the market customers may be those who live within a 2-h drive from the place of business; for accountant, the target market can be within the city limits; and for a consultant, the target market can extend within a five-state region.
- **Customer targeting**: It determine how many businesses or people fit in the customer profile of your business. For instance, a florist may focus on wedding planners in a single region or state while an office manufacturer can target all the retail establishments on office furnishings in a certain region.
- **Product-oriented targeting**: The target market size can be determined by analyzing the types of similar products in the market. For example, a wine brewer can determine the market share as a percentage and all the premium wines sold in the geographic target area.

The market share can be calculated using unit sales and number of potential customers.

- **Unit sales**: This is done by determining the number of products sold yearly. For instance, an entrepreneur in charge of collecting the occupancy tax for the hotels can divide the amount paid by the hotel as tax by the sum of area wide tax collected to determine the market share.
- **Potential customers**: If you know an approximate number of customers in an area, then it is easier to determine the potential market size of your company. For instance, if you know out of 100 people you have approximately 10 customers, then in an area with a population of 5000 persons will present you with 500 clients.
- **Total sales volume**: This entails calculating how much people spend at similar businesses in your target area annually and divide the figure by the amount of the sales, then calculate 10% of the entire market share to be yours. Suppose the Green Stars Landscaping Company serves a market area of 20,000 houses, out of which 10% rely on landscape services. This implies that the potential market for landscape services comprises of 2000 homes. If Green Stars has a 10% market share, then the market size will comprise of 200 homes.

d. Describe your target customers by mentioning your customer segment, their characteristics, and the factors they are likely to consider before purchasing the product;
e. Clearly mention the unit price of the products or services;
f. Forecast the expenses and revenue.
Forecasting the revenue and expenses during business start-up is more of an art than science. Entrepreneurs argue that forecasting is normally time-consuming but investors will not be willing to invest in a business that are unable to give realistic and thoughtful forecasts. Proper financial forecasts are a recipe for development of staffing and operational plans that will ensure that the business is a success.

**Some rules to follow while doing forecasting**

1. **Start with expenses rather than revenues**. During the start-up stage, forecasting expenses is much easier than revenues. Therefore, start by estimating the fixed costs such as rent and utility bills, variable costs such as direct labor costs and costs of goods sold.
**Rules of thumb while forecasting expenses**
    a. Double the marketing and advertising estimates since they always go beyond the expectations;
    b. Triple the estimates for insurance, legal, and licensing fees since their prediction without experience is challenging and in most cases will exceed the expectations;
    c. Monitor the customer service and direct sales as direct labor expense even though you may be doing this by yourself during start-up because as the business grows, you may require forecasting this expense after the client-based expands.

2. **Use both the aggressive case and the conservative case to forecast revenue**. Most entrepreneurs will normally fluctuate between aggressive dream and conservative reality. This keeps them motivated and ready to inspire others. Instead of forecasting revenue based on conservative thinking only, embrace your dreams and establish some projections using aggressive assumptions. This is the only way to think big on how to become big. By establishing both the aggressive and conservative assumptions, an entrepreneur is able to relax on some aggressive cases but force himself through the conservative assumptions. For instance, a conservative assumption may be no sales staff or low price point while an aggressive assumption can be low price point for the base products and higher prices for premium products or two salespersons paid on commission.
3. **Assess the key ratios to ensure sound projections**: It is very easy to forget about expenses after establishing aggressive revenue forecasts. Many entrepreneurs will work aggressively toward achieving the revenue and assume that expenses can be adjusted easily so as to accommodate reality in case the revenue fails to materialize. It is critical to note that the power of positive thinking can help the business in increasing the sales but it is not sufficient to pay the bills.
   Reconciling the expense and revenue projections can be appropriately done through reality checks for the key ratios. Some of these ratios include the gross margins, operating profit margin, and total headcount per client.
   a. *Gross margins*: This is one of the ratios where most aggressive assumptions are so unrealistic. The gross margin reflects the ratio of total direct costs to the total revenue in a certain period. Beware of the assumptions that increase the gross margin from 10% to 50%. If expenses in direct sales and customer service are high, then there is high likelihood that they will be higher at later stages.
   b. *Operating profit margin*: This determines that ratio of the total operating costs to total revenue in a given period of the year. Total operating costs include all the overhead and direct costs less financing. As the revenues increase, the overhead costs should represent a small proportion of the total costs, while the operating profit margins should be on the higher. Most entrepreneurs make a mistake of forecasting the break-even point very early and make an assumption that they do not require much financing to reach there.
   c. *Total headcount per client*: This ratio is especially critical to the entrepreneurs who intend to grow the business on their own. The ratio entails dividing the number of employees by the number of clients and decides on how you want the business managed in 5 years after it grows. If one will not be able to manage the accounts all by himself/herself, there is a great need to revisit the assumptions about payroll or revenue expenses. Establishment of an accurate set of forecasts for a new start normally takes time. Many entrepreneurs regret not spending more time in business planning since they would have avoided incurring so many expenses on their way.

g. Outline the marketing strategy that will be adopted by your business to achieve the sale target. Describe how you will determine the approach to use in potential markets. This includes *promotional strategy* where you mention, what to advertise, *price strategy* outlines the methods to be used in determining the price, the *distribution strategy* that describes how the product/services will be delivered to the client, and *market expansion strategy* that is required to describe any plans for expansion into both the local and international market.

h. Mention the annual marketing budget on how you intend to spend the money for marketing your products.

| No. | Cost element | Budget |
|---|---|---|
| 1. | Promotion costs | |
| | a. Sampling, demos, etc. | |
| | b. Coupons | |
| | c. Price reduction | |
| | d. Free products | |
| | e. Other promotional items | |
| 2. | Distribution of product | |
| | a. Intensive distribution | |
| | b. Elective distribution | |
| | c. Exclusive distribution | |
| 3. | Sales commission | |
| | a. Commission to managers | |
| | b. Commission to salespersons | |
| | c. Commission to merchandisers | |
| | d. Target commission to dealers | |
| | e. Sales commission to shelf boys | |
| 4. | Other promotional costs | |
| | a. Ifthaar party | |
| | b. Lid gifts | |
| | c. New year gifts | |
| | d. Events sponsorship | |
| | e. Other costs (specify) | |
| 5. | **Total annual marketing budget** | |

i. Determine and explain the risks that are likely to affect the business and steps required to mitigate such risks.

j. Assess the seasonal trends that help to come up with the highest and lowest peak seasons.

| No. | Element | Month/Duration |
|---|---|---|
| 1. | Peak season | |
| 2. | Off-season | |

## *Operations Plan*

The operations plan should include the following:

**a.** Stages in production process where the entrepreneur describes the production process, steps involved in production, flow chart, how quality will be maintained, and parameters that need to be checked.

**b.** The implementation of the project should be mentioned where the time allocated for the implementation of the project is outlined.

c. Production capacity should be mentioned.
d. The fixed asset, corresponding costs, and their depreciation should be listed.

| No. | Fixed Assets | Quantity | Rate | Value | Asset Durability | The Year of Depreciation | Depreciation per Year |
|---|---|---|---|---|---|---|---|
| 1. | Land (no depreciation) | | | | | | |
| 2. | Buildings | | | | | | |
| 3. | Machineries and equipment | | | | | | |
| 4. | a. | | | | | | |
| 5. | b. | | | | | | |
| 6. | c. | | | | | | |
| 7. | Furniture and fixtures | | | | | | |
| 8. | Vehicles | | | | | | |
| 9. | Van, trucks, etc., if any | | | | | | |
| 10. | Computers and peripherals | | | | | | |
| 11. | Others (specify) | | | | | | |
| 12. | **Total** | | | | | | |

e. Outline the maintenance and repair costs for the fixed assets and mention their life span and how to maintain their functionality.
f. Outline the annual cost of raw materials where you mention the requirement for raw materials, cost, source, availability, and suppliers among other information (Table 4.1).
g. Describe the workforce to be engaged in production where both the direct and indirect workers are supposed to mention their respective wages and impact of their availability to the production.
h. Describe the factory overhead costs like utilities, depreciation of the fixed assets, rent, repair and maintenance cost, and other costs.
i. Mention the production cost.

**Table 4.1: Projection of Raw Material Consumption**

| No. | Type of Raw Material | From Stock | | Purchases | | Closing Stock | |
|---|---|---|---|---|---|---|---|
| | | Quantity | Value | Quantity | Value | Quantity | Value |
| 1. | | | | | | | |
| 2. | | | | | | | |
| 3. | | | | | | | |
| 4. | | | | | | | |
| 5. | **Total** | | | | | | |

| No. | Element/Description | Reference/ Justification | Cost (yearly) |
|---|---|---|---|
| 1. | Cost of raw materials | | |
| 2. | Cost of goods sold | | |
| | a. Opening stock | | |
| | b. Raw material purchase (added) | | |
| | c. Closing stock (minus) | | |
| 3. | Wages | | |
| | a. Permanent workers | | |
| | b. Temporary workers | | |
| | c. Direct wages (factory) | | |
| | d. Indirect wages (managers, supervisors, administrative personnel, etc.) | | |
| 4. | Factory overhead cost | | |
| 5. | **Total** | | |

**j.** Describe the inventory management and this includes the storehouse, its size, and plans for security maintenance.

## *Management and Organization Plan*

Organizational or management plan is a hierarchical arrangement of responsibilities, authority, rights, and communication of an organization (Baldwin, 2012). For any business,

**a.** organization structure should clearly shown those who will be in management, their qualifications and experience;
**b.** organization of partners/associates should be described briefly;
**c.** succession plan describing the next of keen in absence of the proprietor;
**d.** the cost and activities during the business start-up should be described;

**Startup Activities Budget**

| No. | Business Start-Up Activities | Duration/Time Frame | Cost |
|---|---|---|---|
| 1. | Business plan preparation | | |
| 2. | Registration and license for doing business | | |
| 3. | Loan application, if any | | |
| 4. | Contracts and agreements for starting | | |
| 5. | Purchase of land/building or rent | | |
| 6. | Connection to utilities (gas, electricity, water, phone landline) | | |
| 7. | **Total** | | |

e. list all the office equipments required and the cost of the fixed assets in the office;
f. outline the salaries of the employees;
g. describe the administrative expenses such as stationaries, postage, office utilities, office rent, and entertainment among others;
h. describe any monitoring and evaluation to be put into place. This includes any plans to monitor the progress of implementation and they objectively verify the success indicators for the business;
i. describe the CSR projects that the company is required to undertake to fulfill the responsibility toward community;
j. describe the plans for research and development on any areas or issues that need further analysis or study in terms of current and future success of the business;
k. describe any plans for training and development and the skills that you want to build both to the senior and subordinate team.

### *The Financial Plan*

This section is critical while seeking funding from angel investors, venture capitalists, or even from family members. You should present the numbers in such a way that show the business will grow quickly and there is an exit strategy for the lenders at the horizon where they can make profits. The financial section enables the entrepreneur, understands the business well, and acts as a guide for running the business. The rule of thumb is to be realistic and credible, and you should represent the growth trajectory in an understandable and detailed manner. Break figures into components by target market segment or by sales channels and provide realistic estimates for revenue and sales.

**Following are the components of the financial section**

- **Start-up capital**: The start-up costing sheet should be prepared well before starting the business to give a person, a more realistic idea of how much it will cost. List all the items and their total amounts. Forecasting helps in giving a person an idea of how much the business start-up will cost.
  Following are the costs should be taken into consideration during business startup:
  - Market research on customers, competitors, and products
  - Licenses and permits
  - Registrations
  - Rent
  - Wages
  - Trainings
  - Insurance
  - Printing and Stationary
  - Business assets
  - Others

Thereafter, total all the start-up costs to have a clear picture on the amount of money required for start-up. Whether the business is existing or is a new start-up, an entrepreneur will be required to estimate the actual or approximate figures against each item. Whether you have already started or intending to start, you need to fill in actual or estimated.

- **Sales forecast**: This projects the sales over a period of 3 years on monthly basis.
- **Expense budget**: This estimates how much the business is going to incur to make the sales forecasted. It is critical to differentiate between fixed and variable costs. Low fixed costs imply less risk. Go with simple months.
- **Cash flow statements**: This shows the physical dollars that move in and out of the business. This is partly based on the sales and balance sheet items. For existing business, use historical documents like financial statements while for new start-ups, project the cash flow statements. Ensure you chose a realistic ratio at which the invoices are paid. You can use some business planning software to assist in making the projections.
- **Income projections**: This is a proforma for profit and loss statement that details the forecast of the business in 3 years. Make use of the numbers in sales forecast, cash flow statements, and expense projections.
- **Balance sheet/assets and liabilities**: Set up a projected balance sheet that outlines the assets and liabilities that are unavailable in profits and loss statement. Some only affect the business during start-ups. It is recommended that a person starts with assets then move on to liabilities/debts.
- **Break-even analysis**: This is the point at which the expenses in a business will match the sales volume. A projection of 3 years will be critical in carrying out this analysis. The business will only be viable at a point when the overall revenue will exceed the overall expenses, interest inclusive. This analysis is critical for potential investors as they tend to be attracted by fast-growing business ventures that pay back easily hence good exit strategy.

### *Course of Action*

a. Environmental issues needs to have a well prepared plan to address all the handling or depositing or recycling actions; exceptional cases should be taken into consideration, for example if pollution happens, what can be done. This includes management of wastes, ecological balance, and sustainable management of raw materials. Describe any plans to make use of green technology and energy efficient equipment in operations. Also, note any requirement from ministry of environment and the category of the business based on the location and effects to the environment.

b. Ethical issues should be mentioned to depict actions that are to be taken to ensure that the ethical standards of the business are maintained in terms of fairness in market and monopoly among others.

c. Mention any legal issues involved and how the business is required to comply with the existing policies, regulations, and rules that are directly or indirectly related to the business.

d. Mention any intellectual property issues where the copyright, licensing, and trademark among others are going to be protected.

e. Mention the move toward maintaining good working environment that promotes peace and harmony in workplace.
f. Mention any plans to establish and maintain partnerships with both the investors and stakeholders.
g. Describe all the security and safety issues and measures that the business plans to implement to ensure that all the employees are safe.
h. The plan should mention any ideas for use of IT such as ecommerce, accounting software, or data analysis software among others.

### Conclusion

The business plan should contain a final conclusion. A strong conclusion for a business plan can enhance the support required to grow the business. On the other hand, a weak and uninspired conclusion can make the potential investors to drift away and not dare giving out their cash to support your business. A business plan is hypothetical in nature; therefore, it should leave the investors feeling as confident with the business idea as the owner(s) of the business. A strong conclusion should reiterate the overall vision, make it clear what you require from the reader, and give a call to action that will inspire the readers to join you.

#### *Steps Towards a Good Business Plan Conclusion*

- *Step 1*: The conclusion should be written using an optimistic tone. You should sound like you strongly believe in your company and your idea. For instance, you can start by saying "This plan will be a great avenue for the ABC company to meet its financial goals" rather than saying "if all goes well, ABC company will gain benefit…"
- *Step 2*: Summarize the opportunity by giving a detailed review of information like target demographics, start-up capital, and projections. Give a summary and remind the reader of those details.
- *Step 3*: Give a clear outline of where you intend to be in the next 3 years. Convey a message that the reader will definitely benefit from investing in the company. For instance, you can say "From the projections in this plan, ABC will grow its revenue by 50% over the first 3 years."
- *Step 4*: Give an emphasis of what makes you outstanding among your competitors. Any investor would like to invest in a company with a competitive edge. For instance, you can say "the combination of cutting-edge technology and years of experience of our team, ABC will claim the top most position in the market."
- *Step 5*: Convey a message to the reader that you require them to come onboard. The plan may be exciting to the reader but his perspective of contribution may differ from what you require. Give the exact figure of the investment that you want the reader to give.
- *Step 6*: End with a call to action. Make it clear that you have done your job and since you have told the reader what he/she is expected to do, a final push can seal the deal. For instance, you can end by saying "take this excellent opportunity to get on the ground floor of the company with untapped and unlimited potential."

## Reasons Why Investors Are Reluctant to Finance Some Business Plans

Business plan acts as the first impression that potential investors get about the venture. An entrepreneur(s) can have great product, customers, and team, yet fail to get funded because of some simple mistakes that many people ignore while writing a business plan. Investors receive thousands of business plans requesting for funds. Apart from referrals from their trusted sources, the business plan is the only document that can be used as basis to determine whether or not to fund the business.

With the increasing opportunities, many investors will simply focus on looking for reasons to turn down the request. According to them, observant and keen entrepreneurs will focus on eliminating any mistake that counts against his/her funding.

## Common Business Plan Mistakes

### Content Mistakes

a. *Failure to relate to true pain*: Pain will present itself in many flavors such as computer crashing, too long accounts receivable, or even complex process of preparing tax returns. An entrepreneur is in business to take away the pain and get paid. In this context, pain is synonymous with the market opportunities. The more the pain, the more it will spread, and the better the product will be in removing the pain, hence the greater the market potential. A good business plan will place solution in a firm context of solving the problem.
b. *Inflating value*: Do not use phrases like unique, unparalleled, or any other superb term. In most cases, investors will judge by themselves. An entrepreneur should present the facts and how you intend to stay ahead of the competitors. Ensure that you lay off all the hype.

c. *Do not be everything to everybody*: Most start-ups believe that the "more is better." This makes them explain how the product will be applied to multiple markets. Many investors prefer a more focused strategy, with a single superior product that can solve troublesome problems within a single large market sold through a single and proven distribution strategy. This does not imply that additional applications, distribution channels, products, and markets should be ignored, rather, they should be applied in enriching and supporting the highly focused core strategies. Ensure that you hold the story together with a compelling and strong core thread, which you should identify and let others become supporting characters.
d. *Strategy of no-go-to market*: Any business plan that fails to explain marketing, sales, and distribution strategy is doomed. The plan should clearly outline the people targeted, the reasons why they should buy from you, and how they will access the products. It is imperative to discuss how you have generated the customer interest, obtained the preorders, and made the actual sales. Describe how you intend to leverage this experience in a cost-effective go-to-market stratagem.
e. *There is no competition*: There is no any single business that does not have competitors. The competitor may be an entity that offers identical solution or a substitute. For instance, fingers can be used as substitute for spoon. A first class mail can be considered as a substitute for an email. So, an entrepreneur who says if there is no competition, which portrays lack of understanding of the market and the business plan can be easily tossed off by investors. A competitor is any person who pursues the same customer dollar. The competition section of the business plan presents the entrepreneur with an opportunity to showcase the relative strengths against indirect, direct, and substitute competitors. Besides, competition in business is healthy and is a clear indication to investors that there is existence of a real market.
f. *Lengthy plan*: By nature, investors are very busy with very tight schedules. This implies they have little time to go through a business plan, hence prefer entrepreneurs who can convey the critical elements of a complex idea using an economy of words. For instance, an ideal executive summary should be 1–3 pages and ideal business plan should be between 20–30 pages. Most investors will prefer the lower value of this range. It is critical to note that the main purpose of writing a business plan is to trigger and motivate the investor to invite you to a face–face meeting rather than describing every last detail. The details can be documented elsewhere such as in marketing plan, operating plan, or white papers among others.
g. *Too technical*: Most entrepreneurs with scientific background will in most cases tend to back their plans with complex scientific jargon and technical details. It is imperative to know that investors are interested in your jargons if demonstrate how to solve a big problem that people pay for, is far much better than other competing solutions, is implementable using a reasonable budget, and can be protected through patenting. These can be easily answered without necessarily using complex and technical discussions since the details are reviewed by experts. The business plan should be simple.

h. *Lack of risk analysis*: The aim of investors is to balance risks versus rewards. The first thing that an investor will want to know is the risks that are inherent in the business and any measures that are into place to mitigate such risks. Some of the risks facing entrepreneurial ventures can be related to market, technology, operations, management, or legal. An entrepreneur may feel that the risk is negligible yet potential investors will take it serious unless the entrepreneur demonstrate that the risk has been taken into consideration and prudent steps have been taken to mitigate such risks.
i. *Poor organization*: The plan should have a nice and organized flow with each section building logically on previous sections without necessarily requiring the reader to know the sequence. A good sequence should follow the business plan format presented in this section of executive summary, background, market opportunity, products and/or services, market traction, competitive analysis, marketing and distribution strategy, risk analysis, milestones, management structure, and financials among others. As stated earlier in this chapter, there is no ideal structure that should be followed while writing a business plan. Experiment to find out the best that suits your business.

### *Mistakes of the Financial Model*

a. *Forgetting cash*: Profits, gross margins, and revenues are not cash. Only cash can be regarded as cash. For instance, when you sell a product at $120 and it costs you $80 but you have to pay the suppliers in 30 days and the buyer will pay in 60 days. In this case, the revenue for that month is $120, profits are $40 and cash flow is zero. When you pay the suppliers the following month, the cash flow for the transaction stands at negative $80. This indicates that slight changes in times between receipt and disbursement of cash can easily bankrupt the business. When building the financial model, the assumptions made should be realistic to ensure that the capital raised is sufficient.

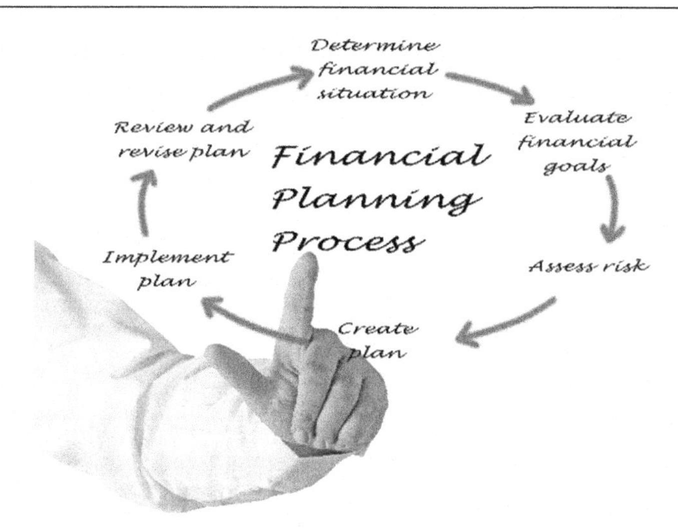


b. *Lack of details*: The financials should be constructed from bottom-up and validated from top-down. In bottom-up approach, the details such as the dates when one expects to make sales or hire specific employees are taken into consideration. The top-down approach entails examining the overall market potential and comparing it to the revenue projections in bottom-up validation. For instance, round numbers such as one million in second year and two million in third year for R&D is a clear sign that the business is lacking a bottom-up model.
c. *Financials that are unrealistic*: It is only very few businesses that are able to achieve over $100 million in sales during the first 5 years of operation. Therefore, projecting more than that is not credible and can get the business plan canned very fast. On the other hand, any business with less than $25 million revenue during the first 5 years may be too insignificant to interest some serious investors. In most cases, financial forecasts will act as litmus test to understand the thoughts of venture capitalists. An entrepreneur with realistic basis of projecting between $50 and $100 million within the first 5 years qualifies for venture financing.
d. *Lack of enough financial projections*: The basic financial projects comprise of income statements, cash flow statements (Table 4.5), and balance sheets (Table 4.4) as the three fundamental components. All these statements should confirm to the generally accepted accounting principles (GAAP). Most investors are interested with 5 year projections as it reflects the thoughtful process that can be used to create some long-term financial projections. Also, a good financial model should have the sensitivity analysis that shows how the projected results can change if the assumptions are incorrect. This is critical to both the investor and entrepreneur as they single out on the assumptions that can have material effects to the future performance of the business so that they can focus on how they can validate those assumptions. Benchmark comparisons should be included compared to

other similar companies to include things like gross margin as percentage of the revenue and various expense ratios among others.

e. *Conservative assumptions*: 99% of entrepreneurs do not believe that assumptions are conservative, though they truly are (Bell, 2014). An entrepreneur should develop assumptions that are realistic and which can be supported.

f. *Valuation offers*: Most business plans err when they state the worth of their company in terms of monetary value. It is critical to understand that the value for a business is determined by the size of the market, and unless one is in business of selling, buying, or investing, it is hard to know exactly what the market bears. Naming a pricing can lead to either of the two things: (1) the price can be too high, hence investors will toss the plan, or (2) the price is too low making the investors take advantage of you. In either way, both are not admirable. The main aim of the business plan is to present your idea in a manner that compels investors to fund you. Prices can be negotiated later.

### Stylistic Mistakes

a. *Spelling and grammar*: Making silly mistakes such as spelling and grammatical errors is a reflection of how one intends to run the business. It is advisable to use spelling and grammar checkers as well using the third party to edit the plan.

b. *Being repetitive*: In most cases, a business plan will tend to cover the same points time and again. An effective business plan should cover the main points only twice: first, in executive summary and second, in the body of the plan while explaining in details.

c. *Appearance*: Most investors will have many plans to go through. An entrepreneur should get to the top by ensuring that the binding is professional, the cover of attractive, fonts are large enough to read easily, and pages are laid out in an orderly manner. Nevertheless, avoid going too far to ensure that you do not give an impression of lacking substance but having the style.

### *Execution Mistakes*

a. *Being late*: The ideal capital formation process takes a minimum of 6 months from the time of writing the plan to the time the money is posted in the bank. The entrepreneur(s) should be ready to invest enough time into the plan. One can consider the option of outsourcing development of the plan if too busy with product, customer base, or company development.
b. *Failure to seek external review*: Ensure that your plan is reviewed to some individuals who have a clear understanding of the market before submitting it. The plan may seem perfect to the development team since they have been having it for months. To get an objective and good review, you can use external parties who have a fresh perspective and can easily save you and the team from myopia.

c. *Over-tweaking*: An entrepreneur can spend a lot of time tweaking the business plan to ensure perfection. Most of the time used in tweaking can be easily used in developing the product, customers, and company. You will be required to, at some point, pull the trigger and present your plan to investors. A positive reaction will be welcomed. If the reaction is negative, get feedback from various investors, go back, and ensure that the plan is refined.

Though the investment climate is currently tough, when good ideas are supported by good business plans and exemplary teams, entrepreneurs will always get funded. It is advisable to give yourself the greatest chance of funding by avoiding the simple mistakes outline here.

## *Sample Business Plan for a New Start-Up*

### *Business Plan for XYZ Cosmetics*

#### *Executive Summary*

XYZ Cosmetics is a company that solves all the needs for cosmetics through manufacturing and distribution of gluten-free products.

Gluten protein is found in barley, rye, and wheat and is very dangerous for people sensitive to celiac disease. Celiac is a major cause for long-term problems such as cancer, infertility, and osteoporosis. The gluten-intolerant persons can be able to improve their lives by eliminating any gluten traces from the food they eat. Today, more than 10% of population in GCC is taking gluten and this has increased the rate of celiac disease by 32%.

The past 3 years have seen an increase in demand for gluten-free food by 33%. Nevertheless, gluten is a hidden threat that lurks in ingredients used in many cosmetics. The gluten can easily get away in cosmetics undetected since companies are not required to disclose the ingredients on make-up labels.

XYZ products offer the best products and we give our clients the freedom to enjoy the luxury of our cosmetics. Unlike most cosmetic manufacturers, we mostly focus on the gluten-free claim and our products are gluten-free certified.

Our target customers are both the organic and natural grocery distributors and stores that are easily reachable through sales programs and trade shows. Most of our end users are ladies aged between 17 and 65 years of age who suffer from gluten allergies. XYZ targets to reach these clients through consumer events, web marketing, and grocery stores to enable them shop easily.

Currently, our fully prototyped lip balm has been receiving positive reviews from friends and families. The eye shadow and mineral foundation prototypes are underway and will be completed in few weeks' time.

We believe that the XYZ products will serve the growing needs for gluten-free personal care and make-up products. XYZ anticipates to break-even in the first year of operations. XYZ will require approximately $50,000 start-up capital.

### *Industry*

XYZ Cosmetics is a component of young niche industry that provides cosmetic products to people who are intolerant to wheat- and gluten-containing products. This market niche is growing at a very high rate and is currently undeserved, hence providing serendipitous opportunity for XYZ.

#### Cosmetic Industry

XYZ Cosmetics participates in the current growing industry of gluten-free products. Currently, the value of cosmetic industry in GCC is over $55 billion. Forbes.com estimates that the global cosmetic industry generates approximately $203 billion annually as sales. Though the industry has been affected severely by recession, there has been strong growth in organic and high-tech sectors.

#### Gluten-Free Cosmetics

The gluten-free industry is relatively young and volatile though the cosmetic industry is stable and mature. Since 2013, the public awareness on gluten-free products has increased significantly.

Gluten protein is found in barley, wheat, and rye. The protein triggers adverse reaction within the body causing nausea, headaches, and debilitating fatigue. Women suffering from celiac disease tend to develop long-term problems upon exposure to gluten. This implies the need to eliminate all traces of gluten to avoid instances of cancer, infertility, and osteoporosis.

Gluten-Free Cosmetics

Despite the increased awareness of gluten-free foods, there has been a notable ignorance to gluten contained in cosmetics. Many people may spend a lot of money to ensure that the food consumed is gluten free yet they ignore the gluten contained in cosmetics. Statistics show that the gluten-containing cosmetics has grown by 43% in the past 2 years.

Cosmetics are largely ignored within the profitable gluten-free products. Currently, only four companies in GCC offer gluten-free certification for their cosmetics. The gluten-free cosmetic industry is still very small when compared to gluten-free food. Gluten is not known to be directly absorbed through the skin. Nevertheless, this can be true for products like lipstick that can be easily ingested. The issue has been glossily covered by the medical practitioners who warn celiac persons the dangers related with ingestion of gluten.

Therefore, consumers can easily reduce the risk of allergic reactions by ensuring that they read the ingredients on all cosmetics and keep tract of the products that have high likelihood of causing problems. Clinical officers recommend that the buyers should be “simple” when searching for new products. XYZ Cosmetics makes the products using simple formulas and allergen-free ingredients alongside full disclosure of the ingredients in the label package. For instance, our lip gloss contain three simple ingredients and our products never cause allergic reactions to our clients since they have been tested and proved to be gluten-free.

According to Beyond Celiac Organization, the celiac disease “is a serious genetic autoimmune disease that damages the villi of the small intestine and interferes with absorption of nutrients from food.” The following selected facts should be noted about the celiac disease:

**a.** It takes up to 10 years for a correct diagnosis of this disease.
**b.** A 100% gluten-free diet is the only existing treatment (there is no pharmaceutical cure).
**c.** Celiac disease can affect men and women across all ages and races.
**d.** About 1% of world population has celiac disease.

*XYZ Cosmetics*

XYZ Cosmetics is involved in manufacturing and distribution of organic and allergen-free personal care and make-up products. Our products are of high quality and are easily distributed online using specialty and natural stores that carry gluten-free products.

The awareness on organic product benefits has increased dramatically over the recent years. Furthermore, many people have been diagnosed with gluten allergies. The research in gluten-free products indicates that many individuals are dissatisfied and confused especially because of the current offerings by the cosmetic industry (Slot & Bremer, 2015).

Our target marketing has been growing at a rapid rate and we have identified our primary markets as women aged between 17 and 65 years of age and who suffer from gluten intolerance. This market niche has a high purchasing power and will normally spend more on any gluten-free product than in any other product. XYZ can easily create barriers to entry by ensuring proper proprietary formulas, superior distribution network, and strong branding.

Background to XYZ Cosmetics

The XYZ Cosmetics is a new start-up, which is to be launched in December 2016.

As XYZ founders, we believe that our passions coupled with our skills are relevant to the XYZ's mission. Ahmed, the Chief Executive Officer, has over 7 years of experience working in food company and has critical information regarding gluten-free products. Fatima is our Chief Operations Officer with extensive experience in chemistry and biology, and this will help in formulation and quality checks for our products. Ahmed and Fatima are willing to work together to launch XYZ Cosmetics.

To date, we have built a website, completed this business plan, conducted beta testing, and prototyped products in our target market.

Value Proposition

XYZ products will offer the consumers peace of mind. Our addition of value proposition will entail the following:

a. Peace of mind where our consumers will be assured that our products are safe to be used without risk of gluten-related side effects.
b. Quality to ensure that our products are both luxurious and effective.
c. Consumer education is by providing materials to consumers on ingredients.
d. Honesty where we will fully disclose our ingredients on the product labels.
e. Purity where we will source raw materials that are of high quality and organic so as to ensure pure products.

### Barriers to Market Entry

The gluten-free cosmetics industry is currently made of many companies and hence barriers will be inevitable though they can be easily handled by determined and smart entrepreneurs. The XYZ is likely to encounter problems in retaining and developing strong wholesale accounts within the specialty and natural grocery. Also, the costs related with raw material sourcing from certified gluten-free suppliers will be substantial. Equipment and manufacturing space may be costly but can easily be lowered by partnering with a third party manufacturer. Such an arrangement can risk contamination with gluten-containing ingredients.

It may take time for XYZ to obtain a consumer brand loyalty since the gluten-free consumers are very sensitive and have found the products that suit them well. XYZ faces a challenge of breaking that loyalty and convincing them to buy their new brand.

Acquisition of certifications such as Gluten-Free Certification Organization may be costly and require period renewals. This can be a barrier against our competitors.

### Key to Success

From the research we have carried out and from our past experience, we believe that any successful gluten-free industry must

**a.** Train consumers on gluten-free products and their advantages;
**b.** Offer a reasonable price point;
**c.** Provide products that are 100% gluten-free;

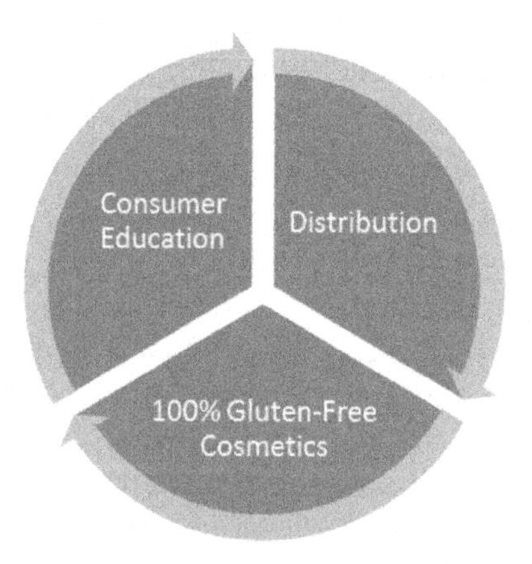


**d.** Keep the consumers engaged through consumer events and social media;
**e.** Create high quality and enjoyable products;
**f.** Innovate frequently to come up with new products;
**g.** Seek for distribution in natural grocery and gluten-free stores.

While XYZ will ensure that the aforementioned success measures are realized, excellence shall be emphasized through three main areas:

a. Consumer education
b. Grocery distribution
c. 100% gluten-free products

*Market Analysis*

Customers

XYZ has identified females aged between 17 and 65 years as the primary market. This will especially target those who are allergic to food, particularly gluten. This customer niche has a very high purchasing power and is accustomed to huge spending on allergen-free foods. The three main factors that will influence the purchase of cosmetics by women include the following:

a. Intense need by women to feel beautiful.
b. Young women have very busy and active lives hence will always seek for products that will contribute to their long-term health.
c. Most middle-aged women will always desire to turn back and become young again. As such, many will tend to spend billions in this pursuit. This implies that the demand for antiaging products will continue growing as Baby Boomers age.

Like most women, our target customers will have make-up to feel young, healthy, and beautiful. Nevertheless, there is still need for products that do not exacerbate their intolerance to gluten. Often, gluten will lurk in unlabeled cosmetics. XYZ offers peace of mind for the certified allergen-free and gluten-free cosmetics.

Market Research

In June 2015, we conducted a small survey to a group of university students. The responses were fresh, natural, wholesome, honest, simple, and clean. Some were fascinated by the design of the website and they confirmed that it was agreeable and comfortable.

Nevertheless, XYZ intends to engage in R&D to ensure continuous improvement of the products and ensure that there is continuous improvement. We acknowledge R&D as a powerful tool that will propel us toward being a market leader in allergen-free, gluten-free cosmetics.

Market Trends and Size

The gluten-free market is expanding at a very high rate. Statistics show that over 18 million people in GCC are gluten intolerant, a factor that has increased the susceptibility to celiac diseases. It is argued that young people have a higher likelihood of contacting celiac disease than it was 30 years back. Therefore, the increase awareness of celiac diseases and related gastrointestinal disorders imply an increase in demand for gluten-free products. The personal care products have the sales reaching up to $6 billion translating to an annual sale rate of 9%.

More than 96% of the gluten-free cosmetics have achieved brand loyalty. Therefore, once XYZ wins the support of the cosmetic users, there will be chances that it will enjoy a long-lasing loyalty from the core customer base.

The consumer awareness on gluten-free products is rapidly increasing and it is anticipated that this will lead to a significant growth within the next 3 years or so. The market is made up of very many small companies and XYZ has an opportunity of dominating the market with a focused message and superior cosmetics.

#### Estimated Market Share

XYZ will primarily gain its market share from mainstream products, which have been crossing over to the gluten-free category. At the moment, many products are not clearly labeled, hence not easily identifiable as gluten-free. This compels consumers to directly contact the company that manufactured the product directly or engage in dangerous guesswork. XYZ will work so as to gain a market share through utilization of unusual go-to-market strategy that targets the distribution through drugstore and grocery channels instead of the normal traditional beauty shops. Furthermore, many companies producing gluten-free products cannot guarantee the user the gluten-free certification. Therefore, having superior convenience, gluten-free certification, and low price points, the XYZ will be able to capture the market and gain a significant percentage of the market share.

#### Competitors

The cosmetic industry is full of small- and medium-sized players. Out of the 18 companies in GCC-producing gluten-free products, only three that are certified as gluten-free. The rest are majorly commanded by the mainstream products that are gluten-free. Our key competitors will be Arbonne, Gabriel Cosmetics, and Red Apple Lipstick. Arbonne has been offering wide range of gluten-free products though their gluten claim is not displayed prominently on the product labels or their website. The Gabriel Cosmetics has been offering a number of gluten-free products though at exaggerrated price. The Red Apple Lipstick has been offering high-quality lipstick, which has a clear gluten-free claim but do not offer any other products apart from lipstick.

From this competitive analysis, we are confident that XYZ has the ability to command the market share in gluten-free niche by ensuring that the products are of high quality and are offered at medium price points. The company intends to become a leader on the market and diversify its offer annually.

#### Differentiation

XYZ is differentiated from its competitors based on the following:

**a.** Having a gluten-free certification
**b.** Relatively lower prices than the competitors

**c.** Full disclosure of the ingredients used
**d.** Education for the consumers

*Marketing Plan*

Market Positioning

XYZ sells its products through ensuring peace of mind to consumers through gluten-free claims. Our products are positioned on a platform of pure ingredients, honesty, and high quality. The brand personality in XYZ is relaxed, friendly, and simple.

Pricing Strategy

The XYZ products will command a medium to high price point, which is relatively better than the competitors.

| Product | MSRP ($)—Manufacturer's Suggested Retail Price |
|---|---|
| Foundation | 29.99 |
| Lip balm | 2.99 |
| Eye shadow | 11.99 |

| Lip Balm: 0.15 oz | | |
|---|---|---|
| Cost per unit | $0.51 | Gross per month |
| Wholesale price | $1.65 | 69% |
| Retail price | $2.99 | 83% |

This price places XYZ products between high end and main stream lip care products.

| Mineral Foundation: 0.3 oz | | |
|---|---|---|
| Cost per unit | $4.48 | Gross per month |
| Wholesale price | $16.55 | 73% |
| Retail price | $29.99 | 85% |

| Eye Shadow: 0.1 oz | | |
|---|---|---|
| Cost per unit | $3.98 | Gross per month |
| Wholesale price | $6.75 | 40% |
| Retail price | $11.99 | 67% |

Due to prototyping, the eye shadow is incomplete and the numbers represented previously are tentative.

The dollar revenue shown is calculated based on wholesale sales. It is anticipated that the direct and online consumer sales will contribute to about 8% of the total dollar volume for the sales. The sales will be at the retail level and will be able to command a high-average net profit margin of about 80% compared to the wholesale average that has a net profit margin of 63%.

### Sales and Distribution

Since XYZ will be selling the products using the primary distribution channels, we will have two different selling cycles. These include trade shows and distribution.

1. *Trade shows*
   In the first year, we will attend the GCC Natural products Expo. The expo will provide an opportunity to create awareness and reach to the largest number of the target customers of the organic and natural products. During the event, XYZ will have the potential of reaching for more than 25,000 industrial players. Due to the high cost related to the event and the relatively low age of our company, we will not attend another trade show in 2015.
2. *Distribution*
   We will be calling directly our gluten-free grocery stores to promote our products. Other consumers will know about our products from the shelves in the local stores.
   Immediately after the start-up, our communication with our clients will be Internet marketing, trade shows, consumer events, and distribution. The main difference will be the quantity of the activities. In the first 5 years, XYZ will ensure a steady increase in marketing budget and will attend to a larger customer base through trade shows and consumer events to drive the growth of revenue.

### Promotion Mix

Our promotion mix will comprise of the following:

**a.** Internet marketing
XYZ will pursue Internet marketing in an integrated approach to drive the customers to the website. This will be achieved through segmenting the clients in terms of age group.

- Customers between 16 and 30 years are considered young and will be reached through social media since they have high likelihood of using a mobile device or a smart phone. The younger population will be reached through market campaigns to create Internet buzz. The market campaigns will be done through Google AdWords, Facebook ads, free giveaway contests, and excellent SEO.
- The client base between 31 and 65 years is considered as middle-aged and will be the largest group of social media users. The group is remarkable in blogging and use of related outlets like Pinterest. The XYZ's SEO and social media efforts will effectively target this group. Also, we will use tactics that involve giveaways and reviews by some influential bloggers.

**b.** Consumer events
The people suffering from celiac are many. XYZ targets to reach this group by using the networks of events and support groups. We aim to reach the consumers by actively participating in consumer events. This will be done by the following:

- Giving support groups free samples and product catalogs;
- Distributing information during the celiac awareness tour and expos;
- Distributing information and sample through doctors's offices and various clinics.

*Operations*

XYZ will be involved in manufacturing, marketing, and distribution of gluten-free cosmetic products. Our products will be of very high quality. The operations model is explained next that we intend to use.

Operations Model

In this model, shows the workflow of operations at XYZ (Fig. 4.1). The tasks in white are primary roles of Fatima while those in green are primary responsibilities of Ahmed.

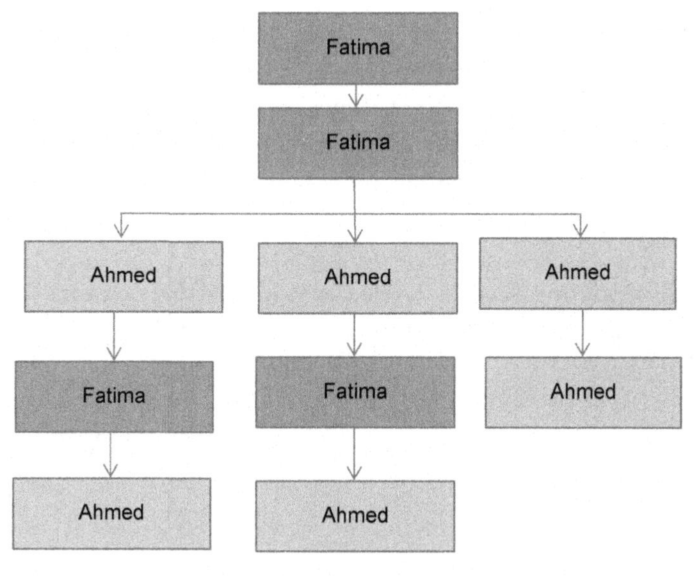


**Figure 4.1**
XYZ operations model.

Facilities and Equipment

Due to the importance of the gluten-free claim to the valuation in XYZ, we feel that it is crucial to ensure that the products are manufactured in-house using dedicated facility that is gluten-free. This is intended to eliminate any possibility of cross-contamination and offer our customers greater peace of mind.

The production and packaging of the products will be done in a dedicated facility by well-trained employees working part-time. Based on a quick survey, we determined the cost of space as between $2.50 and $5.00 per square foot. All the products in XYZ will be manually produced for the early sales and test marketing. Thereafter, quality machinery will be needed, which are relatively expensive. There are two machines that will apply to our process:

a. **Powder compacting machine** with a quoted cost of $71,500
b. **Lip balm filling machine** with a quoted cost of $30,000

During the start-up, XYZ will purchase the machine for filling lip balm, which will depreciated after 4 years. The machine is compact and may not take up large space. Therefore, most of our space will be devoted to storing the ingredients and finish products. Our budget for year 1 estimates an investment of $5000 for the raw materials and total inventory at $4000. The storage will take 15 square feet.

Industrial shelving will be used in storing the inventory. The raw materials and packaging inventory will need 50 square feet. The facility will also contain 30 square feet for working and will have both the hot and cold sinks.

Each of the machine required for the operation will need approximately 50 square feet. Therefore, the total space requirement for shelving, machinery, and work surfaces is 130 square feet. In the first 3 years, the manufacturing will be housed in Ahmed's home. We anticipate that the space requirement will increase with the increase in sales.

Development Status

Our products for initial start-up have been selected using the three criteria shown here:

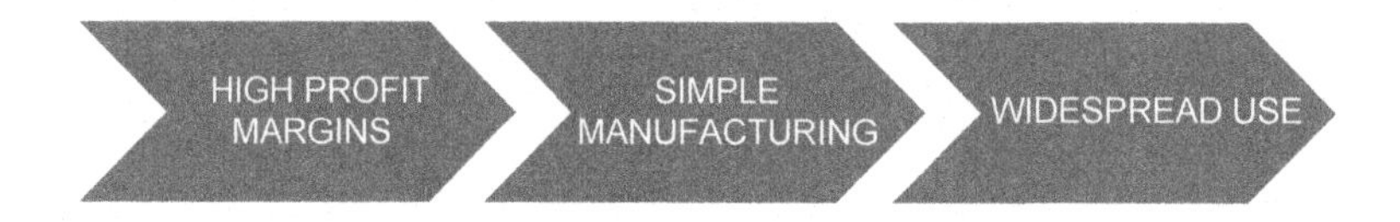


a. *Lip balm*
   Lip balm is a soft and nourishing compound of waxes, flavors, and organic oils. The product is spread over the lips to alleviate chapping as well as add the attractive shine.
   The XYZ lip balm is formulated in a pleasant fresh orange cream flavor. The main ingredients are olive oil, orange extract, and beeswax. Such a simplicity provides a flavor and texture of very high quality. We are in the process of developing additional fruit-inspired flavors in three SKUs (stock keeping units). Currently, we only have 1 SKU of 0.07 oz. The tubes used in packaging lip balm are thin and longer than the standard types, and this creates a unique upscale feel and look.
b. *Mineral foundation*
   This is a soft loose powder with a variety of minerals, oils, and natural pigments and is available in various types of skin tones. The powder is brushed over the skin to give a smooth appearance prior to application of additional makeup.

The XYZ foundation will be formulated in six shades that match various skin tones and will be packaged in 30 g jars. The shelf life for our foundation is 3 years.

c. *Eye shadow*
The eye shadow comprised of pigments, oils, and minerals that are pressed firmly on a small container to form a very soft compound. The product is available in different colors and is blended on eyelid using a small sponge or brush. The formulation of the eye shadow will be in soft pink, blue, and lavender shades. The shades will be sold in singles and in dozen cases. The shelf life for the eye shadow is 3 years.

d. *New products and product improvement*
The XYZ products will be developed in response to the consumer request and trends, as well as through the comments received through social media and emails. This may trigger the expansion of program lines, addition of more products or enhanced R&D for product improvement.

#### Intellectual Property

The XYZ intellectual property will comprise of trade secrets that surround the product formulation and trademarks to protect our brand. The protection of the trade secrets will take place through division of labor and training of employees in the manufacturing department. Our logo trademarks and name will be registered at international level through the attorney and the office for trademark registration immediately after the start-up.

### *Company Structure and Management Team*

#### Human Resources Management

Ahmed Ali and Fatima Mohammed are the founding managers at XYZ.

Ahmed is experienced in gluten-free production as he has worked with a gluten-free food company. He has extensive experience in business management and he holds a degree in entrepreneurship. On the other hand, he is skillful in clinical chemistry, specifically nanotechnology with a strong background in biology.

#### Composition and Ownership of the Management

Ahmed and Fatima are in joint venture and owners of XYZ Cosmetics. The monetary investment is as shown in Table 4.2.

In the first and second year, the founders will be compensated a 12.5% share of the revenue. In the following years, the salaries will be $40,000 and increasing at intervals of $10,000 in subsequent years.

**Table 4.2: Ownership and Management**

| | Amount Invested ($) | Amount Committed ($) | Total ($) |
|---|---|---|---|
| Ahmed Ali | 110 | 4890 | 5000 |
| Fatima Mohammed | 85 | 4905 | 5000 |

### Board of Advisers

Currently, we are in the process of selecting a board of advisors. We anticipate that the board will comprise of knowledgeable individuals who will offer guidance and advice to XYZ Cosmetics. The board will include the following:

- Professor John Harvey: Expert in business planning
- Ann Myers: Owner of Myers Group that manufactures world class surface technologies
- Samira Mahmoud: Student with food allergies and celiac disease
- Bayan Ali: Successful CEO and entrepreneur
- Ali Abubakar: MD of Gulf Snacks with more than 15 years experience in sales
- Maryam Salim: Accounting student

### Plan for Expansion of Operations

Both Ahmed and Fatima will operate the business as a part-time venture in the first 6–12 months. After the break-even point of the venture, the two founders will be working full time.

As the company grows, the gaps in the experience of the founders will be filled by the board of directors who will come on board to offer mentorship services. We are in the process of seeking advisers with experience in R&D and production planning. This is because the two areas are very critical for the success of XYZ and the company will benefit from the expertise of qualified people.

Despite the fact that the founders have strong managerial skills, maximizing growth will require diverse skills. After the first year of operations, XYZ will pursue a more qualified team who has experience and knowledge of different products. We will also take advantage of interns especially during start-up.

## *Critical Risks, Assumptions, and Problems*

This business plan has been based on assumptions, which could be risky if not realized. For instance, we have assumed that there will be a rapid growth in gluten-free cosmetics and that XYZ will be in a position to sustain the demand.

We have assumed that the raw materials will be readily available. Any challenges in sourcing the raw materials and packaging of the finished products may halt the operations in XYZ. Some of the avenues that XYZ should capitalize on to reduce the level of risk include diversification of the supplier relationships.

It is also assumed that XYZ will be able to reach its target customer base to realize the projected sales. Lack of the key distribution channels may imply unsustainable sales. In light of this, we have considered Steve Jones as our advisor on sales.

Legal risks are inherent when producing consumer products such as make-ups. As such, XYZ has plans in place to carry out a general liability insurance. It is also assumed that XYZ is in a position to meet all the standards set by the gluten-free certifications. This will be fulfilled by ensuring that the manufacturing process is simple and the organic ingredients are sourced carefully.

Finally, XYZ anticipates to face challenges in cash flow. This means that the business is at a risk of undercapitalization. We will ensure that the investments during start-up are sufficient. A start-up capital of $50,000 will be enough to alleviate cash flow challenges as the company advances toward maturity. On top of this, XYZ will have a cash flow infusion of $10,000.

### *Financial Plan*

The proforma financials for XYZ are as shown later. The start-up capital of $50,000 will be used in inventory build-up and cash flow as the sales grow to levels that are sustainable.

#### Start-Up Capital

XYZ Cosmetics will start the operations with a $16,950 cash balance, $550 for inventory, and $32,500 for equipment. Here is the breakdown for the start-up capital (Table 4.3).

#### Funding Sources

Currently, we are seeking $28,000 funding. We intend to seek funding from government funding agencies, commercial or Islamic banks, sponsors, business support entities, and/or any other organization.

#### Financial Assumption

Some of the financial assumptions have been made in accounting costs, capital expenditures, computers, cost of goods sold, ending inventory, credit sales, legal costs, insurance, licenses, legal services, online sales, marketing, research and development, purchases, salaries, rent, seasonality, sales, and shipping.

**Table 4.3: Start-Up Capital**

| | **Amount ($)** |
|---|---|
| Capital Investments | |
| Computer equipment | 1500 |
| Manufacturing equipment | 30,500 |
| Other equipment | 500 |
| Operating Expenses | |
| Legal service | **2900** |
| Licenses and permits | 1750 |
| Prepaid insurance | 450 |
| Starting inventory | 600 |
| Cash (working capital) | 11,600 |
| Line of credit annual renewal fee | 200 |
| **Total start-up cash needed** | **50,000** |

Income Statement

| | Year 1 | Year 2 | Year 3 | Year 4 | Year 5 |
|---|---|---|---|---|---|
| Revenue | $91,000 | $191,000 | $343,000 | $551,000 | $775,000 |
| Cost of goods sold | 32,000 | 68,000 | 123,000 | 198,000 | 279,000 |
| Gross profits | 59,000 | 123,000 | 220,000 | 353,000 | 496,000 |
| Operating Expenses | | | | | |
| Salaries | 22,000 | 47,000 | 80,000 | 100,000 | 120,000 |
| Payroll taxes | 2700 | 6200 | 10,000 | 19,000 | 25,000 |
| Office supplies | 600 | 1300 | 2400 | 3900 | 5400 |
| Shipping | 8800 | 18,000 | 33,000 | 53,000 | 75,000 |
| Rent | - | - | - | 4000 | 4000 |
| Marketing and promotions | 13,000 | 28,000 | 51,000 | 82,000 | 116,000 |
| Legal and accounting services | 7900 | 5000 | 7500 | 10,000 | 10,500 |
| Licenses and permits | 1600 | 2500 | 2500 | 2500 | 2500 |
| Line of credit | 150 | 150 | 150 | 150 | 150 |
| Insurance | 2200 | 2200 | 2200 | 2200 | 2200 |
| R&D | 2700 | 5700 | 10,000 | 16,000 | 23,000 |
| Miscellaneous | 2000 | 4000 | 7000 | 12,000 | 16,000 |
| **Total operating expenses** | **63,650** | **120,050** | **205,750** | **304,750** | **399,750** |
| **Net income** | **(4650)** | **2950** | **14,250** | **48,250** | **96,250** |
| **Net profit margin** | **-8%** | **2%** | **6%** | **14%** | **19%** |

Balance Sheet

**Table 4.4: Balance Sheet**

| | Starting | Year 1 | Year 2 | Year 3 | Year 4 | Year 5 |
|---|---|---|---|---|---|---|
| | | Assets | | | | |
| | | *Current Assets* | | | | |
| Cash and cash equivalents | 16,950 | 12,190 | 22,190 | 32,190 | 42,190 | 52,190 |
| Accounts receivable | | 3000 | 13,000 | 23,000 | 33,000 | 43,000 |
| Inventory | 550 | 5632 | 15,632 | 25,632 | 35,632 | 45,632 |
| **Total current assets** | **17,500** | **20,822** | **50,822** | **80,822** | **110,822** | **140,822** |
| | | *Long-term Investments* | | | | |
| Property, plant, and equipment | 32,500 | 32,500 | 32,500 | 32,500 | 32,500 | 32,500 |
| Accumulated depreciation | | 8125 | 16,250 | 24,375 | 32,500 | 40,625 |
| Net | 32,500 | 40,625 | 48,750 | 56,875 | 65,000 | 73,125 |
| **Total long-term investments** | **32,500** | **40,625** | **48,750** | **56,875** | **65,000** | **73,125** |
| **Total assets** | **50,000** | **61,447** | **99,572** | **137,697** | **175,822** | **213,947** |
| | | *Liabilities and Equities* | | | | |
| Current liabilities | | | | | | |
| Accounts payable | 1180 | 2360 | 3540 | 4720 | 5900 | 7080 |
| Line of credit | | | | | | |
| **Total current liabilities** | **1180** | **2360** | **3540** | **4720** | **5900** | **7080** |
| | | *Equity* | | | | |
| Paid in capital | 40,000 | 40,000 | 40,000 | 40,000 | 40,000 | 40,000 |
| Retained earnings | | (5000) | (4900) | (4800) | (4700) | (4600) |
| Total equity | **40,000** | **35,000** | **35,100** | **35,200** | **35,300** | **35,400** |
| **Total liabilities and equity** | **41,180** | **37,360** | **38,640** | **39,920** | **41,200** | **42,480** |

Cash Flow Statement

**Table 4.5: Cash Flow Statement**

| | Year 1($) | Year 2($) | Year 3($) | Year 4($) | Year 5($) |
|---|---|---|---|---|---|
| Operating activities | | | | | |
| Net income | (6000) | 500 | 12,000 | 45,000 | 95,000 |
| Decrease in noncash equivalents | | | | | |
| Accounts receivable | (6300) | (3000) | (8000) | (10,000) | (11,000) |
| Inventory | (1500) | (1600) | (2200) | (2400) | (3400) |
| Increase in cash liability | | | | | |
| Accounts payable | 1800 | 1300 | 2100 | 2500 | 3100 |
| Depreciation | 8100 | 8100 | 8100 | 8100 | - |
| Cash generated by operations | **(3900)** | **5,300** | **12,000** | **43,200** | **83,700** |
| Investing activities | | | | | |
| Purchase of long-term investments | - | - | - | - | - |
| Cash generated by investing | - | - | - | - | - |
| Financing activities | | | | | |
| Line of credit | | | | | |
| Cash generated by financing | - | - | - | - | - |
| Net increase in cash | (3900) | 5300 | 12,000 | 43,200 | 83,700 |
| Cash and cash equivalents at the beginning of year | 16,000 | 12,000 | 16,900 | 28,900 | 74,000 |
| Cash and cash equivalents at the end of year | 12,000 | 16,900 | 28,900 | 74,000 | 156,000 |
| Free cash flow | (3900) | 5300 | 12,000 | 43,200 | 83,700 |

Break-Even Analysis

The break-even analysis is based on the income statement for the first and second years of operation (Fig. 4.2).

The company will break even in November 2016 though during the summer of 2017, income will be negative for a short while after which it will positively increase in Fall of 2017.

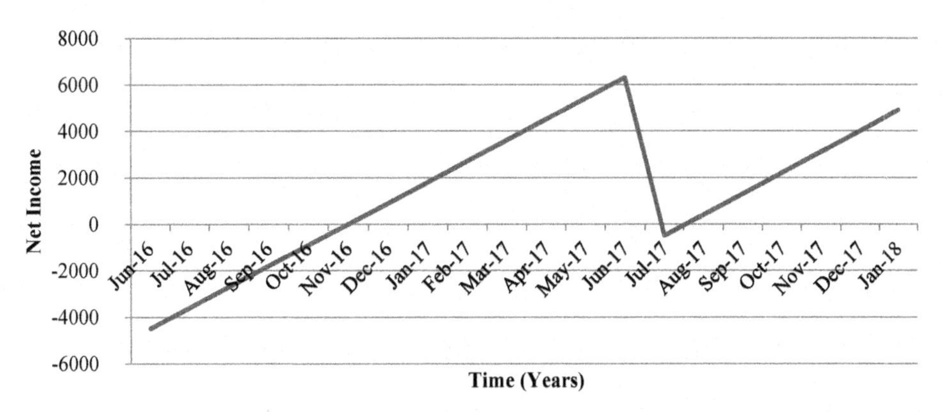


**Figure 4.2**
Break-even analysis.

## Chapter Four Questions

### Choose Either True or False

1. A business plan acts as a road map for the organization, shows the destination of a business, and defines the path to follow to get there.
   - *True*
   - *False*
2. A business plan should be based on the needs of the business and the stage of the business.
   - *True*
   - *False*
3. Business plan is the same as feasibility plan.
   - *True*
   - *False*
4. Any business plan lacking highly detailed and technical descriptions of the product cannot be used to obtain funding.
   - *True*
   - *False*
5. While drafting a business plan, the market share can be calculated using units sales and number of potential customers.
   - *True*
   - *False*
6. Expense budget in a business plan estimates how much the business is going to incur to make the sales forecasted.
   - *True*
   - *False*
7. Cash flow statements present the details on forecasted profit and loss for the business.
   - *True*
   - *False*
8. Balance sheet represents a projected outline of the assets and liabilities that are unavailable in profits and loss statement.
   - *True*
   - *False*
9. Break-even analysis shows the point at which the expenses in a business will match the sales volume.
   - *True*
   - *False*
10. Lack of risk analysis in a business plan may attract investors to fund the venture.
    - *True*
    - *False*

### *Multiple Choice Questions*

11. The following list represents the different types of business plans. Which one of them done when considering a new start-up to evaluate the effectiveness of the idea and whether it is worth pursuing?
    A. Start-up plan
    B. Operations plan
    C. Feasibility plan
    D. Strategic plan
12. Which one of the following is among the reasons why an entrepreneur develops a business plan?
    A. To obtain funding from investors
    B. To define and focus the business objectives in a detailed and comprehensive manner
    C. To act as a selling tool when dealing with prominent relationships such as investors, banks, and lenders.
    D. All of the above
13. Following are the most important components to be included in a business plan. Which one is NOT?
    A. Mission statement
    B. Product/service production process
    C. Business profile
    D. Cash flow assessment
14. Which one of the techniques following is used to estimate the target market?
    A. Unit sales
    B. Geographical targeting
    C. Total sales volume
    D. None of the above
15. Market share can be calculated using various methods. Which among the following is applied when calculating the market share?
    A. Total sales volume
    B. Unit sales
    C. Potential customers
    D. All of the above
16. Following is the list of rule-of-thumb while estimating expenses. Which one is NOT?
    A. Double the estimates for insurance, legal, and licensing fees
    B. Triple the estimates for insurance, legal, and licensing fees
    C. Double the marketing and advertising estimates
    D. Use customer service and direct sales as direct labor expense

17. Following are key ratios used to ensure sound financial projections. Which is NOT?
    A. Gross margins
    B. Return on investment
    C. Operating profit margin
    D. Total headcount per client
18. Which one of the following is not among the components of financial section of a business plan?
    A. Financial control personnel
    B. Break-even analysis
    C. Income projections
    D. Expense budget
19. Which one of the following is among the mistakes when developing a business plan?
    A. Execution mistakes
    B. Stylistic mistakes
    C. Financial model mistakes
    D. All the above
20. A good marketing plan provides a clear concept of the market. Following represent main components of a marketing plan. Which one is not?
    A. Competitor analysis
    B. Profits expected
    C. SWOT analysis
    D. Targeted marketing

**Note: Answers in Appendix section.**

## References

Baldwin, C. Y. (2012). Organization design for business ecosystems. *Journal of Organization Design*, *1*(1), 34–37.
Bell, J. R. (2014). *Think like an entrepreneur*. US: Palgrave Macmillan.
Finch, B. (2013). *How to write a business plan* (Vol. 35). Kogan Page Publishers.
Pauceanu, A. M. (May 2015). Energy management: the path to our future speech. In *Arab renewable energy committee*. Amman, Jordan: AREC.
Slot, I. B., & Bremer, M. G. (2015). Part of celiac population still at risk despite current gluten thresholds. *Trends in Food Science & Technology*, *43*(2), 219–226.

CHAPTER 5

# Understanding the Ecosystem and Starting a Business

## Chapter Outline



**Entrepreneurship in the Gulf Cooperation Council.**

## *Definition of a Business Ecosystem*

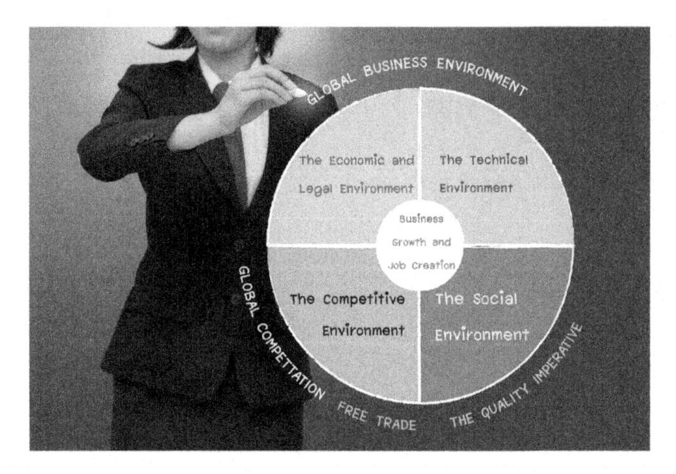


A business ecosystem refers to a strategic planning model comprising of network of distributors, suppliers, customers, and competitors who collectively work together through cooperation and competition to advance sale of services and products (Baldwin, 2012)

Ecosystem is a term that conveys the pieces of economy coming together such that their interactions and strengths form an economic community that determines economic growth and prosperity. An economic community is supported through a platform of interacting individuals and organizations that comprises the major business world organisms (Fig. 5.1).

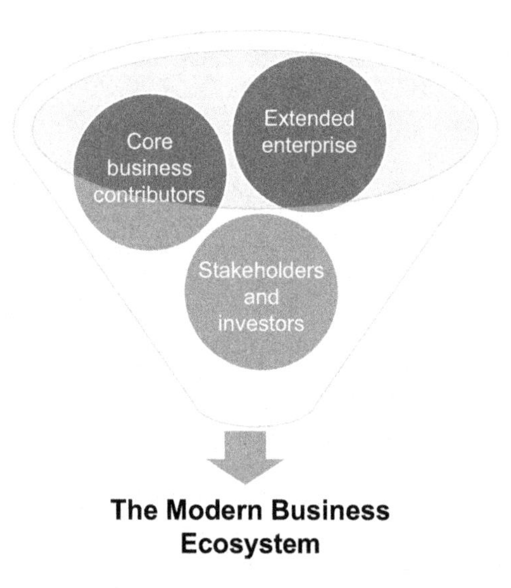


**Figure 5.1**
Business Ecosystem.

The community will produce goods and services that are valuable to clients who are still the members of ecosystem. Overtime, the economic community coevolves its roles and capabilities and tends to align toward the direction established by one or multiple companies. The ecosystem components that hold the leadership roles can change with time but their functions are highly valued by the community as it plays a major role by enabling members move toward a shared vision as well as align their investments and identify mutually supportive roles.

Traditionally, people in any company used to consider other companies as rivals who had to battle each other for dominance and profit. In the current world, organizations operate in a complex relationship where they have to cooperate and compete in unexpected and innovative ways; they need each other for them to succeed. This forms the new world of business ecosystem (the modern concept) and it composed, in the vision of the author, from three elements: (1) extended enterprise components, (2) core business contributors, and (3) stakeholders and investors.

*Extended enterprise elements* are formed from all the other elements, which are not included in the other two sections (for example, nonessential suppliers, professional organizations, regulatory bodies, etc.).
*Core business contributors* are those contributors (suppliers, customers, etc.), which are vital for the existence and success of the organization.
*Stakeholders and investors* are the investors and those stakeholders, which have a major impact on organization's performance and success (for example, managerial team, key employees, etc.).

Pilinkiene and Maciulis (2014), re-analyzing Moore's theory, defines a business ecosystem to include those entities that are considered to be components of a corporation. These include those that are inside the walls of an organization as well as direct suppliers and those in the distribution channels. Also, the ecosystem contains the extend enterprise that comprises of standard bodies, direct customers, the complementary product suppliers among many others. Finally, the ecosystem comprises of those entities that significantly affect the core business but are considered as pesky outsiders or afterthoughts. These comprise of the regulatory bodies, investors, unions, associations, and many others (Glackin, 2013).

Ecosystems have significant implications on how companies plan for their future. Unfortunately, many companies ignore the ecosystems at their own risk. It is critical that businesses and organizations to learn about the business ecosystems and how companies are able to plan for their future. This helps in risk management, improving effectiveness, and acts as breakthrough to new innovations (Finch, 2013).

The purchase power of the local currency has also a major impact on the business environment. It is worth mentioning that the Omani Rial (OR) is strictly paired with US dollar. Nowadays, one Omani Rial equals with 2.59 USD (Pauceanu, 2014).

The recent drastic drop in oil price created a sense of emergency in regard to stimulating entrepreneurial spirit among their citizens and the creation of sustainable development tools (like business incubators, technological parks, free zones, etc.). The Gulf Cooperation Council (GCC) countries are struggling to create a vibrant entrepreneurial ecosystem. There is a need to create a personalized model, especially developed for GCC area. No imitation of any European or American model would fit. To do this, we identified few ideas to be implemented:

- Create own recipe for success, considering specificities of the local culture;
- Listen the successful local entrepreneurs and consider their views, ideas, and suggestions;
- The business centers or entrepreneurship centers need managers with vision who are practically and results oriented and are able to be mentors for potential entrepreneurs;
- Each business center should create and develop a mentoring program.

## Starting Up a Business

Starting a business is a process that entails several things. After coming up with a realistic idea that can be turned into a service or product, there are other factors that should be considered (Parker & Praag, 2012). The modes of starting a business vary in different parts of the world. Though the process is more or less the same, this chapter concentrates on start-up in GCC region, more specifically in Oman.

## Legal Process of Starting Up a Business

### Legal and Regulatory Framework in Oman

The corporate law in Oman stipulates that businesses may be run as private companies, limited liability operations of any other types of concern. In Oman, the legal system is based on both the Islamic Sharia Law and Civil Code Principles. The civil matters originate from the Islamic Sharia and 1996 Oman Basic Law. According to the Basic Law, Islam is regarded as the state religion while Islamic law forms the basis for legislation. The existing regulations and laws remain in force as long as they do not interfere with the provisions of the basic law. According to the provisions of Basic Law, the areas that are only governed by Sharia law are only the inheritance and family law.

The Commercial Court handles the commercial disputes. Since Oman depends on civil law, judges can freely interpret the agreements in their own opinion. This may extend to the amendment of the contract if there is feeling that amendment can accurately reflect the original intentions of the parties.

### Establishing Business in Oman

According to the Ministry of Commerce and Industry (MOCI) from Sultanate of Oman, the following types of business entities can be established in Sultanate:

- Individual firm/merchant
- House trade business (HTB)
- Joint partnership
- Limited partnership
- Limited liability company
- Public joint stock company
- Closed joint stock company
- Foreign company branch
- Commercial representative office
- Commercial agency

It is relevant to mention that HTB, individual firm/merchant, commercial representation office or foreign company branch can be terminated without liquidation. The rest of business entities must pass through the liquidation process accordingly to Omani commercial law (Industry, 2016).

House trade business (HTB) is a small business entity intended exclusively for Omani citizens. No foreigner can establish it and the Omani citizens who are already investors in other companies may not establish it. This type of business is inexpensive and very easy to form and is suitable for home business (home-made sweets or food, handicrafts, perfumes, etc.).

Individual foreign investors and foreign companies can establish operations in Oman through one of the following major forms:

- Joint (public or closed) stock company
- Commercial agency
- Limited liability company (LLC)
- Commercial representative office
- Foreign company branch

### *Limited Liability Company*

Individuals and foreign companies are supposed to have an Omani partner who owns at least 30% of the shares to be registered as an LLC. This is equivalent to a minimum capital share of OMR 150,000 or $390,000 to register an LLC that has foreign partners. The GCC companies that are fully owned by the GCC nationals or the GCC nationals themselves can establish an LLC in Oman without necessarily having a local partner. An LCC should have a minimum of two partners.

Pursuant to the free trade agreement (FTA) that was concluded between Oman and US, the companies from US may establish subsidiaries in Oman without any local partner on condition that all the ultimate shareholders are US nationals. The minimum capital share for LLC with GCC or local ownership, or those that qualify under the US FTA in Oman is $52,000 (OMR 20,000).

### *Joint Stock Company*

The joint stock companies whose shares are not offered for public subscription are said to be privately held (SAOC). The minimum share capital for an SAOC is $1.3 million (OMR 500,000).

Alternatively, the joint stock companies whose shares are offered publicly comprise of the SAOG. The SAOG has a minimum share capital of $5.2 million (OMR 2 million). Also, the 30% local shareholding must be observed when establishing joint stock companies. Stock ownership in SAOG is done through the Muscat Securities Market that is regulated by Capital Market Authority. The foreign investments in both the financial institutions and banks are under the regulation of Central Bank of Oman.

### *Foreign Company Branch*

Foreign companies may register branches in Oman to execute the contract with quasi-government body or the government itself. The registration of a branch is limited to the duration of the existing contract. Nevertheless, special dispensation can be given to allow a company to register a branch without necessarily having an existing contract with the government. This must be approved by the Council of Ministers.

*Commercial Agency*

A foreign company that lacks commercial registration in Oman can conduct business using commercial agents. The agreements are registered formally under the Commercial Agency Law with the MOCI.

*Commercial Representative Office*

Foreign firms may open a commercial representative office in Oman dedicated for marketing and promotion of their services or products. Representative offices are not allowed to engage in any buying, selling, or any other form of commercial activity. Nonetheless, the office can hire or sponsor employees.

*Joint Ventures*

The joint ventures are mainly formed to ensure that foreign countries can benefit from conducting businesses in Oman without having a physical presence in the country and are free of all the risks and costs associated with establishment of legal entity within the country. A foreign country enters into joint partnership with a local company that has at least 30% Omani shareholding. The foreign country will there not be subjected to any registration or licensing requirements.

## Legal Forms of Incorporation

### Limited Liability Company

LLC is one of the common legal forms used in running a business. A company is incorporated to form an entity that has a separate legal personality, and this implies that an organization can engage in a business and form contracts on its own. Upon incorporation, a company is required to have two major constitutional documents. These include the following:

1. *Articles of association*, which represent a contract between the members and the company and they set a legal binding rules for the company and this is inclusive of ownership, control, and decisions. The Company Act of 2006 allows significant flexibility to draw the articles so as to suit the specific needs of the company as long as it is within the law.
2. *Memorandum* that records the fact that the initial subscribers agree and wish to form a company and consequently become its members. It is impossible to amend a memorandum.

A limited company is normally owned by its members who invest in the business and enjoy limited liability. This implies that the company's money is separate from individual money. As a general rule, the creditors of the company can only pursue the assets of the company to settle a debt rather than the personal assets of the owners. Two main mechanisms for company membership include company limited by shares and company limited by guarantee members.

- *Company limited by shares* has each of the members having some shares in the company, hence become shareholders. The limited liability by shareholding implies that the members stand to lose whatever had already been committed to be invested (unpaid amounts on shares) or has already been invested.
- *Company limited by the guarantee members*: A company limited by shares has a voting right attached to each share meaning that the members can vote on important decisions that affect the company. One share is normally equivalent to one vote though this is not the standards. Companies may choose their own class of share and voting rights. The company limited by guarantee has its one-member equivalent to one vote.

Finance for a company limited by guarantee member comes from the loans, members' contribution or retained profits. A company limited by share can raise funds from shareholders in exchange for increased stake in business and any profits are distributed inform of dividends. Limited companies have a higher capacity to finance the business than most of unincorporated companies since they can use the assets held as security for obtaining loans and this gives them charge over their assets.

The limited companies are subjected to stricter regulatory requirements than the unincorporated firms, hence, greater transparency and accountability are vital for members to benefit from the company. Also, accountability is required both from the people dealing with the company and also the shareholders. The company is supposed to comply with the taxation stipulations of the country such as value-added tax, income tax, withholding tax, and many others.

A company that is limited by shares can either be a public limited company (Plc.) or private limited company (Ltd.). The main difference is that a Plc. is allowed to sell shares to the public. Nevertheless, a private limited company forms the most common legal incorporated form of company. Private limited companies may upgrade to Plcs. to take advantage of raining funds. A Plc. is exposed to stricter regulation than their private counterparts so as to ensure protection and transparency of the public investors who are in most cases not included in management decisions of the company.

A Plc. may become a listed company after it floats its shares on a recognized stock exchange. This creates a wider market for its shares. A listed company is subjected to even greater regulations in the form of listing rules as well as the requirements of information disclosure to ensure maintenance of integrity and proper functioning of the market.

### Limited Liability Partnership

An LLP is a corporate body that has separate legal personalities, which are similar to those of a company. The members of an LLP will enjoy limited liability; limited by the amount of money that each person has invested in the business and any other guarantee given to raise the money. Each member enjoys an equal share of the profit unless otherwise specified.

Every member within an LLP is required to register, and both the members and LLP are entitled to take self-assessment returns. The noncorporate members of an LLC are required to pay income tax and the national insurance contributions on the profits. Additionally, the LLPs should file annual returns and file accounts. The LLP should at least two designated members who hold additional responsibilities such as signing off, filing accounts, and appointing auditors.

LLPs enjoy more freedom than limited companies especially in arrangement of the internal affairs and distribution of profits among the members.

### *Intellectual Property Rights*

The intellectual property right refers to the rights given to a person on account of their creativity. The creator is accorded exclusive right over use of their creation for a specified period of time. The intellectual rights are divided in to two major areas. These include the following:

1. Copyright and related rights
   These are the rights accorded to authors of both the artistic and literacy works such as musical compositions, computer programs, sculpture, paintings, and films among others. Even after the death of the creator, the works are normally protected by copyright for 50 years. Also, copyright protects performers, phonogram producers, and broadcasting organizations. Copyright plays a major role is to reward and encourage creativity (Baldwin, 2012).
2. Industrial property
   Industrial property entails two main areas:
   a. The first industrial property right entails protection of the distinctive signs, particularly trademarks, which distinguish goods or services of a particular undertaking from those of others as well as the geographical indications that identify goods that originate from a place where a certain characteristic of good it is attributed to geographic origin. Protection of the distinctive signs helps in stimulating and ensuring fair competition as well as protects consumers by allowing them make informed choices on various goods and services. The protection can last indefinitely as long as the sign continues to be distinctive.
   b. The industrial property rights protect and stimulate innovation, design, and technology creation, hence given incentives and means of financing research and development. A functioning intellectual property regime must facilitate technology transfer in the form of joint ventures, licensing, and foreign direct investment. The finite term for the protection is 20 years for patents.

It is critical to note that the intellectual property rights are subject to exceptions and limitations that help in fine-tuning the balance between legitimate interests of users and holders of those rights.

### Bankruptcy Laws

Bankruptcy laws allow for the elimination or reduction of certain debts and provide timelines for repayment of the nondischargeable debts in a certain period of time. This also permits organizations and individuals repay the secured debts; debts where vehicles and real estates are pledged as collateral and are in most cases favorable to the borrower.

In Oman, bankruptcy laws are mostly ordered by the court based on the initiative of the court after the debtor company or creditors file an application. The courts in Omani appoint administrators to manage the assets of the debtor while the application of bankruptcy is still pending. After a company is declared bankrupt in Oman, liquidation can follow where the court appoints a liquidator to facilitate transfer of the remaining assets of a company. Liquidation is normally done through public auction or judicial sale (Al-Sadi, Belwal, & Al-Badi, 2013).

To distribute the assets of the company that has been declared bankrupt, all expenses incurred by liquidator or administrator, including compensation, are paid from the assets of the company that has been declared bankrupt before making any distribution to the creditors. As a general rule, the debts associated with both the secured and unsecured private debts should not be as high as debts owed to the government irrespective of whether the government debts came later and are unsecured. Unlike the bankruptcy laws in most countries, the Omani laws for liquidation and bankruptcy are straightforward. The laws are aimed at protecting the creditors and ensure efficient liquidation of insolvent company.

## Professional Training and Development Program

Professional training refers to training where a person is taught skills that are relevant to working in a particular profession. This is done via an expert in the field. Nevertheless, attending the trainings is not a guarantee that one will become a professional (Moon, 2013).

Understanding the scope of running a business is critical. The entrepreneurial training program is a powerful resource designed to help one develop a solid knowledge as well as learn what it takes to establish a thriving business. The professional training and development program is important in the following ways:

- Help the entrepreneur put the business idea to test;
- Enhances business plan development skills;
- Increases the capabilities of an entrepreneur in exploring real-world possibilities;
- Increases the chances for success and reduces the costs related to trial and error;
- One is able to get answers to experienced instructors and facilitators.

The trainings and development programs are offered in financial management, legal and risk management, recording keeping and taxes, business plan development, business start-up models, marketing needs and planning, and basic accounting and finance among others.

Most entrepreneurs perceive employee training as optional, a viewpoint which is quiet costly in both long-term and short-term progress of the business. They tend to consider training as more of an expense, hence many companies do not have trainings and development that is focused on producing results for the company. In most cases, business owners will tend to give their people trainings that seem good without necessarily having the objectives of what to get in return. Lack of measurable results implies that the business will always perceive trainings as expenses rather than investment. When training is considered as an investment, there will always consideration on how to get the rate of return on investment, hence triggering the needs analysis (Huber, 2011).

The needs analysis, in the context of training and development, is simply an outcome analysis of what the business owner wants after the training. It is critical for the business owner to ask him/herself what the business will gain from the training. This requires careful consideration where one focuses on processes rather than products. During the needs analysis, one has to focus on strengths and weaknesses of the company and try to determine the existing deficiencies, which if corrected can potential lead to an upward gain in the business. A major area of concern in many companies is training the supervisors to better manage the performance. The promotions to management positions target those people who are technically good rather than those who are capable of helping the subordinates reach their peak performance. The determination of professional training and development requires a need-based approach and establishment of learning dynamism in the company (Hoyle, 2012).

In the current economy, if the business is not learning, then there is high chance that the business will lag behind. A business will learn when employees learn. The employees are critical tools used in producing, refining, protecting, delivering, and managing the products and services. With the increase pace of the 21st century, continuous learning is very important for continued success of the business. To create a learning culture in the business, the business owner should clearly define his/her expectation from the employees and outline the steps required to hone their skills and enable them stay at the top of their fields of work or professions. It is critical to support their efforts by supplying them with necessary resources required to accomplish these goals. Also, communicate with the employees the specific targeted results and training needs you establish through the needs analysis.

The business owner should provide sound orientation and introduction to the culture of the company to any new employee hired. This includes proper training on how to undertake their procedures. A successful training and development program should also include components, which address the current and future leadership requirements. This should provide for a system that identifies the training needs and develops people in a way that ensures the business remains profitable (Harrison, 2011).

The financial considerations regarding trainings can be perplexing through in most cases, the actual budgetary impact is dependent on how the business owner addresses the learning, leadership, and needs analysis. When training is targeted to specific needs, then there is more likelihood for the business to succeed and attain value to whatever was spent on training.

When the training budget fails to have a specific outcome, then there is high likelihood that the money will be spent on courses that are irrelevant to the company.

Most companies have their training budgets as a function of the financial environment: downturn or upswing. During upswing, most companies spend money on irrelevant trainings while in downturns, the trainings may be perceived as very important and sometimes eliminated. In many economic environments, the expenses in trainings should be determined by the business results targeted rather than other factors that are budget-related. To help countering such tendencies, it is advisable that you carefully assess the training and development needs of a business to identify the needs as well as brainstorm on how to achieve the desired results in a more efficient and effective manner (Neck & Greene, 2011).

Employees form the principal business asset. When one invests in them strategically and thoughtfully, the results can be overwhelming and the business can reap rewards, which pay off both now and years to come.

## Sources of Business Financing

The most challenging part in business financing is getting money to kick off. In most cases, an entrepreneur might have a clear and great idea on how to have a successful business but inadequate finance can limit the takeoff. Raising money for start-up requires very careful planning and entrepreneur should know the following:

1. The amount of money required?
2. How and when the money is needed?
3. Is there security for the funds obtained?
4. Is the entrepreneur ready to give up the business control of the start-up in exchange for investment?

The financing needs should take into account the following:

1. Start-up costs, which refer to costs that are incurred before the business starts operating.
2. Starting investment that includes all the fixed assets required before a business can start operating.
3. Working capital, which refers to the stocks required by the business such as allowance amounts after the beginning of sales and raw materials.
4. Growth and development capital for the extra investment in capacity.

Following are the sources of business financing:

### Personal Investment

This is the money invested when borrowing, either in terms of collateral on your assets or in cash. This is an indication of commitment to your project. This is the reason why many lending funds require a small percentage (usually up to 5%) from the potential entrepreneur.

### *"Love Money"*

This refers to money loaned by parents, spouse, friends, or family. Nevertheless, it is critical for an entrepreneur to note that this may not be so much reliable as friends and family will rarely give much capital. Also, they will in most cases want to have equity in the business and an entrepreneur is advised not to give them equity. A business relationship with friends and family should not be taken lightly.

### *Venture Capital*

This is the money that is provided as seed in early business stages. Most of the venture capital funders will invest in a company in exchange for equity. The venture capital investment occurs after the seed funding and is a form of private equity. Venture capital can also be described as a way through which public and private sectors construct institutions that creates network for new industries or firms. The institution helps in identifying and combining the business functions like technical expertise, finance, business models, and marketing expertise. After integration, the enterprise will succeed in becoming nodes for design and construction of products within their domain. In most cases, the decisions by venture capitalists are biased and exhibit some illusion of control and overconfidence, similar to entrepreneurial decisions.

This is the financing that originates from individuals or companies in the business of investment in young and privately held establishments. They give capital to young business in exchange for equity. Normally, the venture capital firms will be unwilling to participate in initial stages of business financing unless the venture has a proven track record of its management. They will in most cases prefer to invest in ventures that already have significant equity investments from the founders and which are already profitable. They prefer business that is highly competitive with a strong value proposition in terms of proven product demand, patent, and protectable or very special idea (Bell, 2014).

The venture capitalists will in most cases take a hand-on-approach on their investments, where they require to be presented in board of directors and even in hiring of managers. They can be instrumental in providing business advice and guidance. Nevertheless, they will always be substantial returns for their investments and sometimes their objectives may cross with those of the founders since most of them are focused on short-term gains.

Most of venture capital firms focus on creation of an investment portfolio with businesses that have high growth potential and which will in most cases result to high rate of return. Most of such businesses are highly risky. The venture capitalists may target annual returns of between 25% and 30% on the overall investment portfolio. Since the businesses they interested in are highly risky, they will prefer investments with at least 50% expected returns. Some business may give at least 50% returns while some will not. As such, they hope that the investments will have a 25–30% returns (Boohene, Ofori, Boateng, & Boohene, 2015).

The venture capitalists believe in 2-6-2 rule of thumb, which implies that two investments tend to yield more returns while six will yield their original investment or moderate returns and two will fail. It is good to note that funding may not necessarily be available for all entrepreneurs. Most venture capitalists target technology-driven businesses as well as companies with high growth potential in areas such as biotechnology, information technology, and communications.

The venture capitalists will tend to take an equity position to enable them execute a highly risky but promising venture. This may entail giving up equity or some ownership of your venture to an external party. The venture capitalists will always expect healthy returns on investment, which is in most cases generated when the business offers shares for sale to the public. Ensure you look for investors who will bring relevant knowledge and experience to your business (Baldwin, 2012).

### *Angels Investors*

These are wealthy retired company executives or individuals who will directly invest in small firms owned by other people. In most cases, these leaders in their field, who contribute their experience, network of contacts, management, and technical expertise. Angels will finance the business during the early development stages.

In return, the angel capitalists reserve the right to supervise the management practices of the company. In concrete terms, this involves sitting in the board of directors as well as taking part in any process that relates to business transparency. They will in most cases tend to keep a low profile and to meet them, one has to contact special websites or specialized associations (Yalcin, 2014).

## Government Funding

Bring innovations that the government fund is not easy. The government funding is critical in covering the expenses like equipment, research and development, marketing, and improvement of productivity and salaries. The government will in most cases offer grants and subsidies. Grant refers to the money conditionally given to the business where one does not have to repay. Nevertheless, one is bound legally to make use of it under the terms and conditions of the grant, failure to which one has to repay. Once a business is granted money from one source of the government, it is possible to receive further funding from the same source upon meeting the requirements of the program.

1. *Direct Grant*: Getting grants is not easy and will in most cases involve strong competition and complex criteria for award. Generally, most grants will require the business owner to match the funds that are being given and the amount may vary considerably based on the granter. For instance, a grant to carry out a research may require the person to just look for 30% of the total cost and the rest is given out.
   a. Requirements for government grants
   b. Detailed description of the project
   c. Explanation of the project benefits
   d. Detailed work plan with clear costs
   e. Detailed presentation of background and experience of key managers
   f. Filled application forms.
2. *Soft loan*: Soft loan is an example of grant where the conditions of repayment are lower than in normal financial circumstances. For instance, the government may charge little or no interest rate and repayment periods could also be longer.
3. *Equity finance*: This refers to the capital that is injected into a business by the government after which it gets an equity in the enterprise. After the firm increases in value, the government can withdraw. Unlike the venture capitalists, equity finance has less strict terms.
4. *Subsidized/free consultancy*: This is a business support service offered for free or at subsidized rates by the government for the firms intending to start up and they lack certain skills to run the company.

## Bank Loans

A loan refers to credit, usually in form of cash that a person borrows and repays over the agreed period of time. The banks can offer loans to business. Nevertheless, for start-ups, banks are very hesitant in giving out loans unless there is evidence of existing assets or good credit history.

Some of the advantages of bank loan are that they are repayable in a whole term rather than on demand like overdrafts. It is also easy to tie a loan to lifetime of the asset or equipment you are borrowing the money for, and finally, the bank does not demand a share of the profits or company. Nevertheless, loans are not flexible where one has to pay charges when repaid early or fines when repaid late. When loans are taken against assets as security, there are chances that the assets can be sold upon failure to comply with the payments. Also, payments for loans with variable rates can change and this may make it hard to pay for the finances.

In GCC, we can find two types of financing:

- Islamic financing, through Islamic banks or divisions of banks; Islamic financing is governed by Sharia law, the main characteristic is that there is no interest for the borrowed money but there are other fees included;
- Commercial financing, through commercial banks.

The fundamental distinction between commercial banking and Islamic banking is the contractual relationship. In the traditional (commercial) banking system, the contract between a customer and a conventional bank is simple; a loan where interest is charged upon, usually as percentage (fixed or floating). In Islamic financing, the financial arrangement is based upon partnership, profit sharing, buy and sell, etc. The Islamic financial loan is more expensive than the commercial loan.

## Infrastructure

Infrastructure remains a critical component of economic development. Effective and efficient infrastructure is critical in promoting economic growth and competitiveness. The development of infrastructure promotes productivity, communication, production, and transportation. The quality and accessibility of infrastructure is critical in shaping the investment decisions of domestic firms and will in most cases play a major role in attracting investors (Rietveld & Bruinsma, 2012).

The Omani's most visible investment in infrastructure has been in highways and roads. Overall, the new infrastructural development in Oman coupled with the cheap labor and probusiness policies has made it an attractive hub for foreign direct investment (FDI). GCC is working hardly in this regard and the results are visible. All GCC countries have a clear vision for development for the next 20 years.

### Investment Opportunities in Gulf Cooperation Council

#### Free Zones

In Sultanate, there are three economic (free) zones. These include the Salalah, Sohar, and Al Mazunah, as well as Duqm, which is a special economic zone. Sohar is fully exempted from customs duties on all the imported goods. The businesses in this area can be 100% foreign owned while the tax exemptions are up to 25 years. The Sohar Industrial Estate within Sohar is a free zone reserved for food, steel, and logistics sectors.

Salalah Free Zone (SFZ) is in the southern side of Oman. The zone offers competitive infrastructure and labor costs so as to attract investors in material and chemical processing, assembly, and manufacturing. The income tax exemption is up to 30 years. There is allowance for full foreign ownership without minimum capital stipulations for setting up the company.

"Salalah Free Zone is a location with cost competitive market reach and access in a country that has a business oriented environment" (Zone, 2016). This business-oriented environment has a visible impact also in the local community. SFZ is supporting and encouraging locals to establish small businesses and serve the companies established here (catering, transportation services, typing services, etc.). In this circle, the community receives a growth stimulus, which contributes to a sustainable local business environment and sustainable community. Being very near to Salalah port, it offers a competitive advantage for the business entities established here.

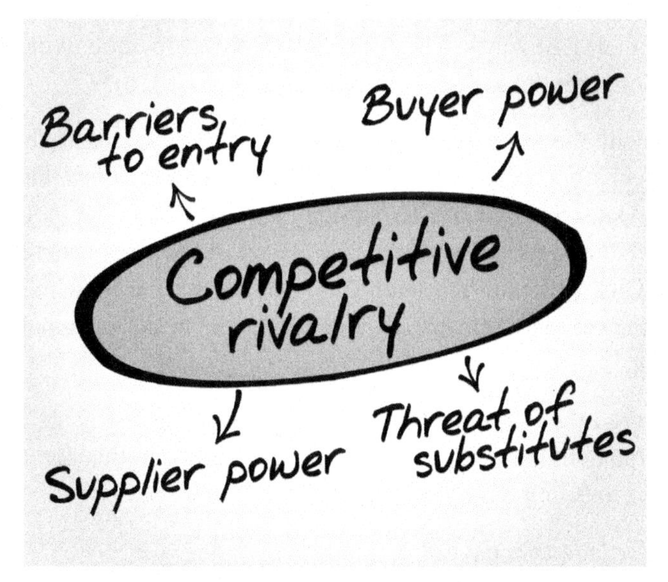


"Salalah does not just provide port advantages but an entire suite of opportunities that when combined create a true value proposition like none other in the region" (Port, 2016). To bring its own contribution toward sustainable development of local community, Salalah port has adopted an acquisition policy, which gives priority to local businesses, in the way that when the port needs supplies, they will search first on the local market and in case they will not find what they need will expand its search nationwide or international. In the image beside is presented porter's five forces model in evaluating the business environment within one country.

Al Mazunah Free Zone is in Dhofar region in south western parts of Oman. The one is reserved for light industry, trading, and assistant services sectors. The income exemptions in this zone are up to 30 years. Customs exemptions are available and full foreign ownership is allowed.

There is no limit for minimum capital requirement for setting up the industry. The Yemeni nationals are allowed to work in this zone without necessarily having work permits or visas.

The Duqm economic zone is at the Arabian Sea coastline and serves as a gateway to and a major hub for North and East Africa, Middle East, and South Asia. Duqm has several areas such as tourism and educational sections, logistics and industrial sections, petrochemicals and filter complex, town, and airport. Some of the incentives offered to investors in this area include competitive rates for leasing lands and 30 years' income exemption plus full customs exemptions. There is allowance for 100% foreign ownership. It is important to mention that Chinese investors are extremely interested in this specific area.

The free zones in UAE are the most attractive ones for foreign investors. These zones offer 24-h time frame to establish legally your company (Jebel Ali free zone for example) and very little bureaucracy for the investor. UAE is the leader among GCC countries in attracting foreign investors for their free zones. They offer also a one-stop-shop, which serves efficiently all the needs of potential investors (UAE Free Zones, 2016).

Qatar is the country with the fastest growing economy and this fact is visible in its efforts to establish business incubators, technological parks, and economic zones. One of the most efficient free zone is Qatar Science and Technology Park (QSTP). The industrial areas within the county are Doha Industrial Estate, which is set to serve medium-scale and light industries; Mesaieed Industrial City, Dukhan Petroleum City, and Las Laffan Industrial City, which are based around hydrocarbons and industry, playing a key role in the sustainable growth and development of Qatar.

Qatar leaders understood the importance of attracting foreign investments and developing through entrepreneurial activities. They are a tough competitor in this regard for UAE and they are working hard to become the leader in GCC.

*Public Establishment for Industrial Estates*

Public Establishment for Industrial Estate (PEIE's) main purpose of existing is to attract foreign investors in Sultanate and to work on localizing the national capital in specific areas of interest. From this main purpose, other interests are derived:

- Active contribution toward sustainable economic, environmental, and social development in Sultanate;
- Establishing and reinforcing collaboration with regional and international entities, for knowledge and experience exchange, common projects, and common interests;
- Focusing on developing specific economic sectors in Sultanate including transportation, tourism, banking, etc. (Public Establishment for Industrial Estates, 2016).

In 1983 in Rusayl, the first industrial estate was established, and PEIE was established 10 years later. There is a 5 years tax holiday for all industrial estates, and it can be renewed for other 5 years. For the purpose of attractive foreign investors, Sultanate offers a variety of incentives for investors. Sultanate is the only country from GCC, which offers export credit insurance through Oman Development Bank's Export Guarantee and Financing Unit (EGFU), which contributes significantly to export increment and is a major incentive for investors.

## *Industrial Parks*

An industrial park, also known as trading estate or industrial estate, is a section that is set aside, planned, and zoned for the purpose of industrial development. It can be considered as a heavyweight version of an office/business park (Dong, Geng, Xi, & Fujita, 2013). Most industrial parks are normally located outside of main residential areas and have good infrastructural access. Most industrial parks are located close to transport facilities such as railroads, ports, airports, and highways. Some of the reasons for setting aside industrial parks include the following:

1. To enhance dedicated concentration of infrastructure in an area so as to reduce the business expenses related with infrastructure;
2. To attract new businesses through provision of an integrated infrastructure in a location;
3. To reduce the environmental impacts of industrial wastes.

Some industrial parks may offer incentives to the members such as financing in tax increment and customs exemptions.

In Sultanate of Oman, the most representative technology park is Knowledge Oasis Muscat (KOM), established in 2003 in Muscat. KOM is the symbol of "successful public–private partnership in nurturing knowledge-based businesses" (Knowledge Oasis Muscat, 2016). KOM aims to become a leader in the region as a promotor of entrepreneurial activities, excellence, and creative innovation.

In the United Arab Emirates, Masdar city (the free zone and the science and technology park) is internationally recognized to be the most sustainable and eco-friendly one. The investors benefit from various incentives and are complemented by the state-of-the-art infrastructure. It also provides a one-stop-shop eServices (Masdar City Free Zone and Science & Technology Park, 2016).

Another representative technology park from UAE is CERT Technology Park. It was developed with the main purpose to encourage and promote the technological exchange and expertise within the international business community. CERT Technology Park and its partners provide a wide range of mutually beneficial services, which are fostering the technological transfer (CERT, 2016).

In Qatar, the most representative is QSTP. QSTP is part of Qatar Foundation Research and Development and aims to grow Qatar's "postcarbon economy" (Qatar Science and

Technology Park, 2016). QSTP is also Qatar's primary incubator focusing mainly on supporting innovation and entrepreneurship and accelerating commercialization of research. It is a tool which is contributing to the fulfillment of some of Qatar National Vision 2030's goals in this regard.

## *Technology Parks and Business Incubators*

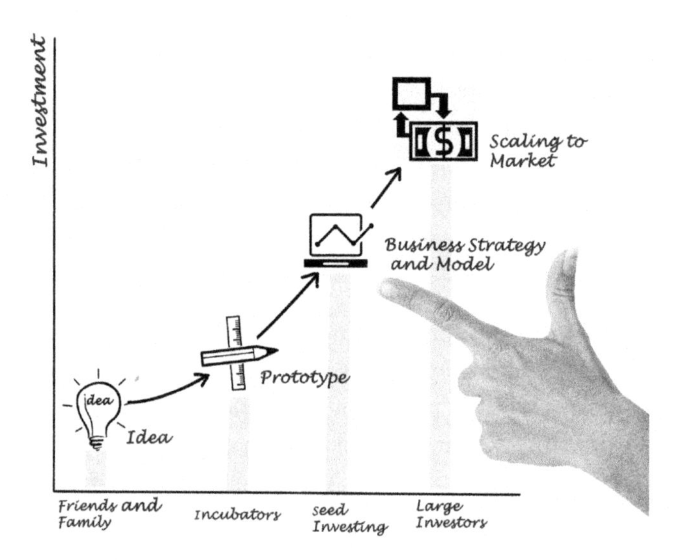


Business incubators are usually referred also as business accelerators. It is necessary to make a clear distinction between a business incubator and business accelerators.

According to Gil Silberman, "incubators provide a physical office space, networking opportunities, and basic business services (IT, janitorial, conference rooms), whereas accelerators offer free or bundled professional services (strategic consulting, management coaching, branding, PR, fundraising, design) and virtual/contract management teams" (Quora, 2016). Whatever someone call them, incubators and accelerators, these two sustainable development tools are vital factors of companies' growth, be it from early start-up or in becoming established organizations.

In regard to GCC area, being in the initial phase of development, there is need of business incubators, at least one in each region. Using now the accelerators would lead to very quick growth and development, which is not sustainable.

Their major focus is in high-tech sectors where they provide support for new businesses in different development stages. Also, there are local incubators for economic development whose main focus is in sectors such as revitalization and hosting, job creation, and service sharing (Bøllingtoft, 2012). For instance, an incubator may allow use of own laboratory for development of a new product so that the new business can start testing its product cheaply before the start of any production. The incubation phase for start-ups may last up to 2 or 3 years. The business can leave the premises of incubator (the incubation phase) and becoming independently (Al-Mubaraki & Busler, 2011).

Businesses receiving such kind of support will, in most cases, operate in state-of-the-art sectors like information technology, industrial technology, multimedia, and biotechnology. The success rate of the business supported through incubator is at least 5 years (there will be a 2 years follow-up process once the business launch itself by its own).

On the other hand, a technology park offers opportunity for development of large-scale projects and do not offer any business assistance services that are a hallmark of business incubators. Nevertheless, many technology parks will house the incubation programs. In author's opinion, each technology or industrial park should have a business incubator within, for providing complete range of services and contributing to start up success. If 5 years ago, the normal tendency was toward specialized business incubators, nowadays, within the world's economic context, there is a need for mixed-use incubators.

GCC area and Sultanate of Oman are in urgent need of customized business incubators, which will contribute to the sustainable development of business ecosystem and increase the number of SMEs (Pauceanu, 2016).

In the United Arab Emirates, one of the most successful business incubator is Silicon Oasis Founders (SOF). SOF is belonging to UAE government through Dubai Silicon Oasis Authority. The expertise of this entity is to help emerging entrepreneurs creating their business plans and launch their business (Silicon Oasis Founders, 2016). Other successful business incubators in UAE are Impact Hub Dubai, AstroLabs Dubai, In5 Dubai, Seed Startup, etc.

UAE has established few accelerators, which still have a long run ahead. The most representatives are TURN8 Dubai and Flat6Labs Abu Dhabi.

In Qatar, one of the most successful business incubators is Qatar Business Incubation Center (QBIC). It has a 2-year incubation process for start-ups and they follow the entrepreneur from the beginning. They offer two types of incubation programs: direction incubation and lean start-up program. After the incubation period, QBIC support remains available for the companies as follows:

- For location (space), it can be used for another 12 months, and
- Assistance or guidance for another 6 months (Qatar Business Incubator Centre, 2016).

It is worth to mention here Qatar University Business Incubator and the Digital Incubator, the last one belonging to the Ministry of Transport and Communication.

**SWOT Analysis of the Business Environment in Sultanate of Oman**

| Strengths | Weaknesses |
|---|---|
| · Very secure area, no threats of terrorist attacks (zero risk estimated by international agencies)<br>· Positive and stable international commercial relations with free trade among GCC countries<br>· Free trade agreement with USA and Singapore<br>· Well-developed banking system<br>· Several business opportunities in various fields (e.g., tourism, renewable energies, medical, etc.)<br>· Good infrastructure<br>· Young demographic—almost half of the population is under 25 years with an increasing level of literacy<br>· Stable government and strong support for private sector investments<br>· Economy has solid potential for further development and growth<br>· Plenty advantages for foreign investments in the free zone areas with 100% foreign ownership<br>· Low level of taxation and even tax exempt for long time for free zone investments<br>· Exporting goods and services produces in the free zones without any tax<br>· No tax on repatriation of capital<br>· 5% Sale tax for the goods/services produced in the free zones and which are sold on the local market<br>· One-stop-shop for foreign investors who would like to settle their businesses in the free zones<br>· Investor-friendly environment and modern business law framework<br>· Modern ports with modern infrastructure for transportation of goods all over the world<br>· No risk of expropriation | · Language barriers<br>· Lack of public transportation system<br>· Sultanate is still developing from technological and infrastructure point of view<br>· Difficulties in obtaining work visas for workers from outside of Sultanate<br>· High level of bureaucracy and lengthy procedures for foreign investors<br>· Strict work regulations and conditions for expats<br>· Lack of short-term specialized training courses for the workers<br>· Locals prefer government jobs instead of private sector<br>· Lack of marketing and efficient promotion channels<br>· Lack of local specialized work force<br>· Conservative country system<br>· Small domestic market<br>· High staff turnover<br>· Discrepancies in regional development |
| **Opportunities** | **Threats** |
| · The Omanization process<br>· Better and efficient management of cultural and natural resources<br>· Great interest from international investors<br>· Plenty of historical and cultural places, providing growth opportunity for touristic demand growth<br>· Promotional activities on behalf of the country from the Ministry of Tourism, opening offices in different countries and participating at various exhibition's events ("Oman—Beauty has an address")<br>· Cost competitive advantage to enter on markets as USA or Singapore (due to the free trade agreements) | · The Omanization process<br>· Lack of environmental monitoring and active measure for environment and historical places' protection and prevention of pollution<br>· Risk of very rapid growth with its consequences<br>· The Omani rial is strictly paired with US dollar (1 omani rial equals 2.58 USD, fixed exchange rate), so there is a risk that if the US dollar weakness will lead to imported inflation;<br>· Government initiatives are not coordinated from a centralized office so delays or discrepancies may occur<br>· High level of competition (to attract foreign investments) with other GCC countries, which offer excellent incentives and facilities |

**Note**: The Omanization process, which is enforced by the government, at the same time, is an opportunity and a threat. It is an opportunity because the companies must give preferences to Omani nationals even if they are not as well prepared as other expats, so it is much harder for the companies to hire expats, and a threat because most of the Omanis prefer to work for the government and not for the private sector, or prefer not to work until they will find a government job.

*Adapted from Pauceanu, A.M, (2016). Foreign investment promotion analysis in Sultanate of Oman – the case of Dhofar Governorate.* Journal of Economics and Financial Issues*; Pauceanu, A.M., (2014). Strategies for improving the performance of firms operating in Oman tourism industry.* Journal of Contemporary Management Sciences, *3(1), 1–11. JCMS Publication.*

## *Chapter Five Questions*

### *Choose Either True/False*

1. A business ecosystem refers to a strategic planning model comprising of network of distributors, suppliers, customers, and competitors who collectively work together through cooperation and competition to advance sale of services and products.
   - *True*
   - *False*
2. Many companies have been very keen on their business ecosystems as they are well versed with risk management, improving effectiveness, and acts as breakthrough to new innovations.
   - *True*
   - *False*
3. In Oman, the legal system is based on both the Islamic Sharia Law and Civil Code Principles.
   - *True*
   - *False*
4. Finance for a company limited by guarantee member comes from the loans, members' contribution or retained profits.
   - *True*
   - *False*
5. Limited companies have a lower capacity to finance the business than most of unincorporated companies since they cannot use the assets held as security for obtaining loans and this gives them charge over their assets.
   - *True*
   - *False*
6. LLPs enjoy less freedom than limited companies especially in arrangement of the internal affairs and distribution of profits among the members.
   - *True*
   - *False*
7. The intellectual property right refers to the rights given to a person on account of their creativity and can either be copyright or industrial property right.
   - *True*
   - *False*
8. Bankruptcy laws allow for the elimination or reduction of certain debts and provide timelines for repayment of the nondischargeable debts in a certain period of time.
   - *True*
   - *False*

9. Entrepreneurial training is a powerful resource designed to help one develop a solid knowledge as well as learn what it takes to establish a thriving business.
   - *True*
   - *False*
10. Most of the venture capital funders will invest in a company in exchange for equity.
   - *True*
   - *False*

### Multiple Choice Questions

11. Ecosystems have significant implications on how companies plan for their future. Which one of the following is not a function of business ecosystem?
    A. Help in risk management
    B. Improves company's effectiveness
    C. Help in choosing the best management team
    D. Acts as breakthrough to new innovations
12. Individual investors and foreign companies can establish operations in Oman various forms except in one of the following. Which one is it?
    A. Limited liability company (LLC)
    B. Commercial representative office
    C. Branch
    D. None
13. Which one of the following is not a legal form of company incorporation?
    A. Limited company
    B. Limited liability partnership (LLP)
    C. Free zone
    D. All of the above
14. Which of the following is not true about the intellectual property rights?
    A. Intellectual property rights are independent of exceptions and limitations
    B. Copyright is the right accorded to authors of both the artistic and literacy works
    C. Industrial property right protects distinctive signs, particularly trademarks
    D. Industrial property rights protect and stimulate innovation
15. Which one of the following is true about bankruptcy laws?
    A. Bankruptcy laws permit organizations and individuals repay the secured debts
    B. Bankruptcy laws in Oman are ordered by the court before the debtor or creditors file an application
    C. After a company is declared bankrupt in Oman, liquidation should be done away with
    D. The expenses incurred by liquidator or administrator during liquidation process is paid by the company doing the liquidation

16. Which one of the following is not a role of professional training and development program?
    A. Help the entrepreneur put the business idea to test
    B. Enhances business plan development skills
    C. Increases the market size of the company
    D. Increases the chances for success and reduces the costs related to trial and error
17. What is Love Money in business financing?
    A. Money invested when borrowing, either in terms of collateral on your assets or in cash
    B. Money loaned by parents, spouse, friends, or family
    C. Money that is provided as seed in early business stages
    D. Money gotten from wealthy retired company executives or individuals
18. What is venture capital?
    A. Money invested when borrowing, either in terms of collateral on your assets or in cash
    B. Money loaned by parents, spouse, friends, or family
    C. Money that is provided as seed in early business stages given in exchange for equity
    D. Money gotten from wealthy retired company executives or individuals
19. Following are the different forms of government funding. Which one is not?
    A. Direct Grant
    B. Soft loan
    C. Bank loans
    D. Equity finance
20. Following are some of the main reasons for setting up industrial parks. Which one is not?
    A. Enhance a dedicated concentration of infrastructure in an area
    B. Attract new businesses through provision of an integrated infrastructure
    C. Reduce the environmental impacts of industrial wastes
    D. None of the above

## References

Al-Mubaraki, H., & Busler, M. (2011). The incubators economic indicators: mixed approaches. *Journal of Case Research in Business and Economics*, 1–12.

Al-Sadi, R., Belwal, R., & Al-Badi, R. (2013). Woman entrepreneurship in the Al-Batinah region of Oman: an identification of the barriers. *Journal of International Women's Studies, 12*(3), 58–75.

Baldwin, C. Y. (2012). Organization design for business ecosystems. *Journal of Organization Design, 1*(1), 34–37.

Bell, J. R. (2014). *Think like an entrepreneur*. US: Palgrave Macmillan.

Bøllingtoft, A. (2012). The bottom-up business incubator: leverage to networking and cooperation practices in a self-generated, entrepreneurial-enabled environment. *Technovation, 32*(5), 304–315.

Boohene, R., Ofori, D., Boateng, B. D., & Boohene, K. A. (2015). Information and communication technology usage and small and medium-sized enterprises growth in the Accra Metropolis. *Journal of Business and Enterprise Development, 5*(1), 101–110.

CERT. (May 10, 2016). *CERT*. Retrieved from http://www.certonline.com/certtechpark.html.

Dong, H., Geng, Y., Xi, F., & Fujita, T. (2013). Carbon footprint evaluation at industrial park level: a hybrid life cycle assessment approach. *Energy Policy*, *57*, 298–307.
Finch, B. (2013). *How to write a business plan* (Vol. 35). Kogan Page Publishers.
Glackin, C. (2013). Entrepreneurship. *Starting and Operating a Small Business*, *3*, 23–28.
Harrison, R. (2011). Learning and development. *Development and Learning in Organizations: An International Journal*, *26*(1), 302–320.
Hoyle, E. (2012). *World yearbook of education 1980. The professional development of teachers* (Vol. 42). pp.101–105.
Huber, S. G. (2011). The impact of professional development: a theoretical model for empirical research, evaluation, planning and conducting training and development programmes. *Professional Development in Education*, *37*(5), 837–853.
Industry, O. M. (April 16, 2016). *Easy invest*. Retrieved from MCI OM https://www.business.gov.om/wps/portal/ecr/services/faq/commercialregistry.
Knowledge Oasis Muscat. (May 10, 2016). *KOM*. Retrieved from http://www.kom.om/About-KOM.
Masdar City Free Zone and Science & Technology Park. (May 10, 2016). *Masdar city*. Retrieved from https://www.abudhabi.ae/portal/public/en/business/business_support_and_advice/business_information_studies/gen_info100?docName=ADEGP_DF_359500_EN&_adf.ctrl-state=18ffz8h9rv_4&_afrLoop=8160508967695999#!.
Moon, J. A. (2013). *Reflection in learning and professional development: Theory and practice*. Routledge.
Neck, H. M., & Greene, P. G. (2011). Entrepreneurship education: known worlds and new frontiers. *Journal of Small Business Management*, *49*(1), 55–70.
Parker, S. C., & Praag, C. M. (2012). The entrepreneur's mode of entry: business takeover or new venture start? *Journal of Business Venturing*, *27*(1), 31–46.
Pauceanu, A. M. (2014). Strategies for improving the performance of firms operating in Oman tourism industry. *Journal of Contemporary Management Sciences*, *3*(1), 1–11 JCMS Publication.
Pauceanu, A. M. (2016). Foreign investment promotion analysis in Sultanate of Oman – the case of Dhofar Governorate. *Journal of Economics and Financial Issues*.
Pilinkiene, V., & Maciulis, P. (2014). Comparison of different ecosystem analogies: the main economic determinants and levels of impact. *In: 19th International Scientific Conference Economics and Management 2014 (ICEM-2014)* (Vol. 156). pp.365–370. Retrieved from: http://www.sciencedirect.com/science/article/pii/S1877042814060248.
Port, S. (April 16, 2016). *Salalah port*. Retrieved from http://www.salalahport.com/index.php?itemid=148&newsid=86.
Public Establishment for Industrial Estates. (May 9, 2016). *Public establishment for industrial estates*. Retrieved from PEIE http://www.peie.om/.
Qatar Business Incubator Centre. (May 10, 2016). *QBIC*. Retrieved from QBIC http://www.qbic.qa/.
Qatar Science and Technology Park. (May 10, 2016). *QSTP*. Retrieved from http://www.qstp.org.qa/.
Quora. (May 9, 2016). *Quora*. Retrieved from Quora https://www.quora.com/What-is-the-difference-between-startup-incubators-and-accelerators.
Rietveld, P., & Bruinsma, F. (2012). *Is transport infrastructure effective? Transport infrastructure and accessibility: Impacts on the space economy*. Springer Science & Business Media.
Silicon Oasis Founders. (May 10, 2016). *SOF*. Retrieved from http://www.siliconoasisfounders.com/.
UAE Free Zones. (May 10, 2016). *UAE free zones*. Retrieved from http://www.uaefreezones.com/.
Yalcin, S. (2014). SMEs: their role in developing growth and the potential for investors. *CFA Institute Conference Proceedings Quarterly*, *31*(3), 7–11.
Zone, S. F. (April 16, 2016). *SFZCO*. Retrieved from Salalah Free Zone http://www.sfzco.com/en/salalah/why-invest.

# Appendix 1

**Business Model for Small Businesses in GCC**

| Your Business Partners | Resources and Activities | Added Value for Your Customers | Distribution Channels and Categories of Customers | Your Network and Marketing/ Advertising | Financial Reports Income and Costs |
|---|---|---|---|---|---|
| Your business partners can be any of the following:<br>• Suppliers<br>• Acquired resources<br>• Potential partnerships (your motivation behind it)<br>• Your main customers<br>• Other vital elements or partners which might contribute to your success | You should consider at least the following elements:<br>• Your distribution channels (how you will reach your customers)<br>• Your customer relations and how you will deal with them, including complaints)<br>• Physical, human, financial, or intellectual resources<br>• Activities or processes that contributes to making things different from competition | You should consider the following:<br>• What is the customer's need that you are going to fulfill<br>• The value that you deliver to your customers | You should consider the following:<br>• Classify your categories of customers based on the relevance to your income<br>• Evaluate the distribution channels and the best way to reach your target customers<br>• Consider using AIDA model of communication in interacting with your customers | You should consider the following:<br>• Your personal and social networking coverage<br>• The way you will make customers aware of your products/ services and advantages they can get from and buying from you | You should consider the following:<br>• All the ways in which you can get money for your company<br>• Your cost structures<br>• Cost and price value of your company's products or activities |

# Appendix 2

## Answers

### *Chapter One Answers*

1. True
2. True
3. True
4. False
5. False
6. False
7. False
8. False
9. True
10. False
11. A. Decision-making
12. C. Protection of the most valuable assets
13. A. How attractive is the market for the new product/service
14. B. Become risk takers
15. C. Resilience, creativity, and optimism
16. D. Political stability
17. B. iv, vii, vi, iii, v, i, ii
18. C. Entrepreneurs should not be connected
19. B. Political instability
20. D. Employing someone to manage your finances

### *Chapter Two Answers*

1. True
2. False
3. True
4. False
5. True
6. True
7. False

8. True
9. True
10. False
11. C. Profitable
12. C. Medium enterprises as having up to 100 employees
13. B. Bank loans
14. A. Increased interests by potential investors in tech-based or digital ventures
15. B. Reduction in exports
16. D. Poor legal ownership of local businesses due to increased entry of expatriates
17. D. Chasing away the expatriates
18. A. Omani locals register as business owners but are agents of expatriates
19. C. Social
20. C. (A and B)

### *Chapter Three Answers*

1. True
2. True
3. False
4. False
5. True
6. True
7. False
8. True
9. True
10. False
11. A. Operational feasibility
12. D. All the above
13. B. Selling the idea to other well-equipped developers and monitor it
14. D. (A and B)
15. C. Estimation of target customer base
16. B. Validation of the underlying premise for the product/service idea
17. D. None
18. A. Evaluating the projected rate of return of the venture
19. D. All the above
20. A. After idea inception but before developing a business plan

### *Chapter Four Answers*

1. True
2. True
3. False

4. False
5. True
6. True
7. False
8. True
9. True
10. False
11. C. Feasibility plan
12. D. All of the above
13. B. Product/service production process
14. B. Geographical targeting
15. D. All of the above
16. A. Double the estimates for insurance, legal, and licensing fees
17. B. Return on investment
18. A. Financial control personnel
19. D. All the above
20. B. Profits expected

### *Chapter Five Answers*

1. True
2. False
3. True
4. True
5. False
6. False
7. True
8. True
9. True
10. True
11. C. Help in choosing the best management team
12. D. None of the above
13. C. Free zone
14. A. Intellectual property rights are independent of exceptions and limitations
15. A. Bankruptcy laws permit organizations and individuals repay the secured debts
16. C. Increases the market size of the company
17. B. Money loaned by parents, spouse, friends, or family
18. C. Money that is provided as seed in early business stages given in exchange for equity
19. C. Bank loans
20. D. None of the above

# Index

'*Note:* Page numbers followed by "f" indicate figures, "t" indicate tables and "b" indicate boxes.'

Waiting is an entrepreneur's biggest mistake.

Printed in the United States
By Bookmasters